Mastering New Testament Facts

PROGRAMMED READING

ART AND ACTIVITIES

TESTS

to get it all down PAT

BOOK 3
The Pauline Letters

Madeline H. Beck
Lamar Williamson, Jr.

Sketches
KATHY REAGAN
PHIL KESTNER

JOHN KNOX PRESS
ATLANTA

Scripture quotations are from the Today's English Version
of the New Testament. Copyright © American Bible Society 1966.

International Standard Book Number: 0-8042-0328-8
   © John Knox Press 1973
2nd printing 1977
Printed in the United States of America

PREFACE

Mastering New Testament Facts is a guide for both individual and group study of the New Testament. While it has been designed for individual use, it is also easily adapted for use by study groups or classes.

Suggestions for Individual Study

The approach followed in *Mastering New Testament Facts* is one which uses recently developed learning methods. Some of these may seem to be unfamiliar at first, even though they have been used successfully both in public school education and in industry. For example, the suggestion that the student take a pre-test before he has begun to study certain chapters may seem to be an unnecessary or perhaps even an unfair step. However, it has been found that a pre-test on unfamiliar material is often helpful. Pre-tests serve to alert the student to key questions. They are basically previews which help the reader learn the material faster. All of the techniques used in this study are ways of preparing or reinforcing one's memory.

It is very important for the student to read each set of instructions carefully. If the instructions should occasionally seem to be unclear, he might wish to share his questions about them with other students or with a teacher. As this volume has not been designed as a commentary or an interpretation of the theology of the New Testament, the reader may wish to supplement it with such resources as *The Layman's Bible Commentary*, *The Interpreter's Bible*, a good Bible dictionary, or an atlas. *Good News for Modern Man* (Today's English Version) is the most helpful translation of the New Testament to use with *Mastering New Testament Facts*. However, other versions of the New Testament may be used if *Good News for Modern Man* is not available.

Suggestions for Group Study

There are a variety of ways in which *Mastering New Testament Facts* can be used in group study, and each group is encouraged to work out its own procedure. The following ideas may offer suggestions.

1. Each participant in the study should have his own copies of *Mastering New Testament Facts* and *Good News for Modern Man* (Today's English Version).

2. The leader or chairman should help the participants with directions in the book that might not seem to be clear.

3. Regular opportunities for individual study should be included. Thus a class may agree for the individual study to be done outside of the class time. In this case, an agreement or covenant may be adopted regarding the amount of time to be spent or the amount of material to be covered. Other groups may discover that they work best by the concentration of individual study at one class meeting and the use of alternate meeting periods for general discussion. A third approach might be to use approximately the first half of each class period for individual work and the remaining half for discussion.

4. In order to stimulate discussion, the participants could mark on scratch paper or in the margins of their New Testaments the ideas in the passage that seem to be important. A class can devise its own symbols for marking these ideas. These could be quite simple, such as E--exciting, P--puzzling, D--disturbing, H--helpful.

5. If the class is large, it might be wise to divide it into groups of fifteen or fewer for discussion.

6. The discussion may be quite informal and free flowing. On the otherhand, it could be slightly directed. Some classes may wish to discuss first the ideas which seem to be exciting or helpful; others may wish to turn to those which are troublesome as a way of beginning the discussion.

7. The interpretation of a passage of Scripture is often related to particular concerns faced by the church at critical times in its history. Thus the class may enjoy discussing the meaning of a passage for earlier generations. It may also wish to discuss the bearing a passage has on situations faced today in the church, community, or world at large.

8. If the meaning of a particular passage remains difficult to grasp, someone in the class may wish to look for additional resources or further information.

9. Ideas which may work well with one class may not work at all with another. Therefore, each class should feel free to develop its own use of the book, realizing that it should balance discussion with time for individual study.

ACKNOWLEDGMENTS

The development of this course was made possible by the generous support of the Presbyterian School of Christian Education in Richmond, Virginia. President Charles E. S. Kraemer and Dean Malcolm C. McIver, Jr., made staff time and materials available and supported the project with their interest and encouragement.

Outlines of the Pauline Letters have been developed after consulting many other minds. Donald Gutherie, *New Testament Introduction* (Downers Grove, Ill.: Intervarsity Press, 1970) and Willi Marxsen, *Introduction to the New Testament* (Philadelphia: Fortress Press, 1968) have been particularly helpful. The basic structure of Second Timothy was suggested by Mr. Paul Berge, a graduate student at Union Theological Seminary in Virginia.

Professional readers of portions of the course included Prof. James P. Martin, Miss Gay Mothershed, Miss Peggy Ross, and Prof. Richard N. Soulen.

Volunteers for trial testing of an early draft included students at P.S.C.E., Union Theological Seminary in Virginia, Randolph-Macon College, the University of Richmond, Virginia Commonwealth University, St. Catherine's School of Richmond, and members of Westminster Presbyterian Church, Richmond, St. Thomas Episcopal Church, Richmond, and Westover Hills Presbyterian Church, Little Rock, Arkansas. Mrs. Annette Dew of Richmond worked through all four books. Comments and suggestions from these readers and volunteers contributed greatly to the present form of the course.

Typists of original drafts were Sally Lockhart and Jane E. Miller of P.S.C.E. and Mrs. Ruth K. Parrish.

To all of these collaborators in the production of this course, the authors express their deep and genuine gratitude.

CONTENTS

    Before You Use This Book.................................... 1
    The Pauline Letters: Introduction............................ 4

UNIT 1: THE BASIC LETTERS

    Objectives and Pre-test...................................... 5
    Introduction... 9
    Instructions.. 10

Guided Reading: Romans, 1 Corinthians, 2 Corinthians, Galatians... 11

Section Test 1: Romans... 38

Section Test 2: 1 Corinthians.................................... 40

Section Test 3: 2 Corinthians.................................... 41

Section Test 4: Galatians.. 43

Unit Test.. 46

Unit Growth Record... 49

UNIT 2: THE PRISON LETTERS

    Objectives and Pre-test..................................... 51
    Introduction.. 55

Guided Reading: Ephesians, Philippians, Colossians, Philemon...... 57

Section Test 1: Ephesians.. 79

Section Test 2: Philippians...................................... 81

Section Test 3: Colossians....................................... 83

Section Test 4: Philemon... 84

Unit Test.. 88

Unit Growth Record... 91

UNIT 3: OTHER LETTERS

       Objectives and Pre-test...................................... 93
       Introduction... 99

Guided Reading: 1 Thessalonians, 1 Timothy, 2 Timothy, Titus,
                Hebrews..................................... 101

Guided Reading: 2 Thessalonians.................................. 111

Section Test 1: 1 Thessalonians, 2 Thessalonians................. 126

Section Test 2: Pastoral Letters (1 Timothy, 2 Timothy, Titus)... 128

Section Test 3: Hebrews.. 130

Unit Test.. 133

Unit Growth Record... 136

BEFORE YOU USE THIS BOOK . . .

You can save yourself a lot of time by reading carefully the next three pages.

Description: This study guide to the New Testament appears in four books and has been designed to help you learn the content and structure of the New Testament in the shortest possible time. The books are:

>   I. *Introduction and Synoptic Gospels*
>   II. *The Fourth Gospel and Acts*
> III. *The Pauline Letters*
>   IV. *The General Letters and Revelation*

All four books use the PAT system (Programmed reading, Art and activities, and Tests), which enables the student to get the facts down pat.

Uses: If you do the entire course, it will prepare you to interpret any part of the New Testament in the light of all the rest. It will provide the basic acquaintance with the New Testament which is necessary for an intelligent reading of scholarly works about the New Testament. It may be particularly helpful for church school classes or Bible study groups which seek a guide to the New Testament that leaves to the student full freedom of theological interpretation and historical perspective. Newly elected church officers, church school teachers, and candidates for ordination can use this course to review New Testament content.

Any one volume of the series will serve these functions for one portion of the New Testament. Specific objectives are listed at the beginning of each unit in the course.

Learning Process: Mastery of this material proceeds through five stages—one diagnostic, and four learning and evaluative. It is the student's responsibility to see that sufficient review takes place to ensure mastery at each stage beyond the first.

Stage 1: Diagnostic Unit Pre-test

Before you begin a unit of work, you will take a pre-test to measure your present mastery of the facts and skills taught in that unit, and to become acquainted with the types of questions and information you will be learning.

While a "pre-test" may sound strange, you will soon find that it is a help to you. It's not an evaluation but a way of learning, so don't be disturbed that you do not know the material. If you already know it, you do not need to study it.

By taking a pre-test, you will understand the objectives better, you will be more alert to the kinds of information you should remember, and you will have had practice in the kinds of questions you will be using for self-evaluation later.

Then, by comparing the results of your pre-test with those of a unit test after your study, you will be able to see just how much progress you have made by studying the unit. This growth is in knowledge only. The program does not attempt to provide for or measure any growth in faith or development as a Christian. It is up to the individual to use this information as he thinks best.

Stage 2: Guided Reading

You will be asked to read a chapter or so at a time in the New Testament. Outline headings of each book are given in larger type, with major divisions in ALL CAPITAL LETTERS and major subheadings Initially Capitalized. Learning these headings will facilitate your memory of the content of each book and your understanding of the structure and relationship of the parts. As you read the passage under one heading and answer the questions, you will be expected to remember the heading and the major facts in that section.

Buildings, columns, and other appropriate forms represent the outline headings in Units 1 and 2. As the first outline heading is introduced, the first level of the appropriate symbol, labeled with the heading, appears on the right side of the page. By following the growth of this drawing, you will learn the structure of the Letter.

Periodically you will be referred to a section chart and asked to complete a visual book outline, thereby seeing each passage in relation to the rest of the book.

As you read the passages, a series of questions will call your attention to the portions of text that you need to remember. You should silently answer these questions as you read. Answers appear on the back of each page of questions. It is not usually necessary for you to give the exact wording in order to be correct. These questions and answers are only to guide your study.

Sketches, which will help you remember the facts by emphasizing main ideas, accompany most answers in the guided reading. They also summarize the distinguishing features of some books at the end of the guided reading. Take time to associate the sketches with the material you have just read. They reveal more than words and are easier to recall.

Stage 3: Section Tests

Each fact, relationship, or skill that is emphasized in the guided reading or text will be tested in a section test. Section tests are organized into categories of facts to be mastered. You are given help in computing your scores for each category and for the complete test. As you complete the Unit Growth Record, you will see your progress in each area. If you score less than 90 percent on any part of the section test, you should review the relevant material in the study guide and in the New Testament.

Stage 4: Unit Test

When all sections have been completed at the 90-percent level, you are ready to begin the unit test. Once again you will be measured on your mastery of each fact, relationship, and skill taught in the sectional guided readings. You are given help in computing your scores for each category and for the entire test. By comparing your unit test score with your pre-test score you can easily determine your growth during the study of the unit.

Stage 5: Study References

Scripture references are given for all unit test answers. By checking the references for any items you missed on a unit test, you can complete your mastery of this unit's content. If you score less than 90 percent you should review any areas of weakness before proceeding to another unit. This does not apply if your growth from the pre-test was more than 70 percent.

NOTE: This course was designed to be used with *Good News for Modern Man: The New Testament in Today's English Version*, and its language is generally used. However, equivalent terms are used interchangeably to help you accustom yourself to terms you will meet in other books. (Examples: letter/epistle; general/catholic; mighty works/signs.)

THE PAULINE LETTERS
INTRODUCTION

The nine Letters to the churches, the three pastorals, and Philemon were all originally attributed to Paul. Now many scholars question the authorship of some of these, but all agree that they express Paul's theology. Even Hebrews was attributed to Paul for a long time, although it does not express his views. More than any other New Testament epistle, Hebrews stands alone; so it has been kept in canonical order and included with the Pauline writings to which it was sometimes thought to belong.

Although the study guide will use "letter" and "epistle" interchangeably, some of the New Testament epistles (such as Hebrews) are not really letters, but are closer to a sermon or tract or congregational rule book. "Letters" is used here in its canonical sense, not its technical one.

Of the thirteen Pauline Letters, nine are addressed to churches and four to individuals. The Letters in this book can be grouped as follows:

<u>The Basic Letters</u>
1. Romans
2. 1 Corinthians
3. 2 Corinthians
4. Galatians

<u>The Prison Letters</u>
1. Ephesians
2. Philippians
3. Colossians
4. Philemon

<u>The Earliest Letters</u>
1. 1 Thessalonians
2. 2 Thessalonians

<u>The Pastoral Letters</u>
1. 1 Timothy
2. 2 Timothy
3. Titus

<u>The Letter That Stands Alone</u>

Hebrews

The pastoral epistles were written to give guidance to the ministry of the church. These and some of the Letters to the churches may not have been written by Paul but they express and develop his theology. The appearance of Paul's name does not settle debates about authorship because in antiquity a disciple would sometimes honor his teacher by writing in his name. This book reports such debates, but leaves any judgment on the questions to the reader's prior conviction or further study.

All Letters by Paul himself date from the last fifteen years or so of his life at most, about A.D. 50 to 65.

 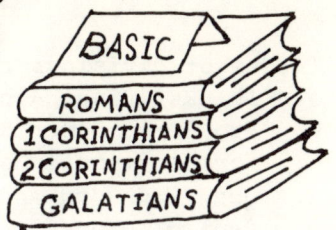

UNIT 1: THE BASIC LETTERS

OBJECTIVES

After completing the study of Unit 1 you will be able to do the following:

1. State the names of the basic Letters of Paul.
2. State the major headings of each of these Letters.
3. Identify Paul's purpose in writing each of the four Letters.
4. Complete portions of 33 major teachings of Paul through answering multiple choice and matching questions.
5. Identify 25 features as distinctive of a particular basic Letter.

The Unit 1 Pre-test will tell you how much of this material you already know. You are not expected to do well on this test because you have not yet studied the material.

PRE-TEST FOR UNIT 1: BASIC LETTERS

A. STRUCTURE: Circle the letter of the ONE BEST answer for each.

1. The major divisions of the Letter to the Romans are:
   a. Doctrine and Ethics
   b. Problems and Answers
   c. Plans, the Gospel, Paul's Concerns
   d. Doctrine, Appeal, Exhortation
   e. Rules for Behavior, God's Love, Products of the Spirit

2. The first part of Romans has these two subdivisions:
   a. Justice and Mercy, Abraham's Doubt
   b. Thanksgiving, Appeal
   c. Prisoners Led in Victory, Duty to the State
   d. Put Right with God Through Faith, Promises to Israel
   e. Food Offered to Idols, Resurrection of the Dead

3. The major divisions of 1 Corinthians are:
   a. Man's Sin, God's Plan, Life in the Spirit
   b. Thanksgiving, Judgment, The Promise
   c. Thanksgiving, Exhortation, Offering to Jerusalem
   d. Disorders, Answers to Questions, Worship
   e. Opening, Doctrine, Conclusion

4. The major divisions of 2 Corinthians include:
   a. Doctrine, Appeal, Exhortation
   b. Paul's Autobiography, Corinthian Response, Paul's Plans
   c. Paul's Message and Mission, Offering to Jerusalem, Harsh Letter
   d. Doctrine, Ethics
   e. Disorders, Warnings, Appeal

5. The major divisions of Galatians are:
   a. Thanksgiving, Appeal, Exhortation
   b. Problems, Doctrine, Thanksgiving
   c. Formal Report, Appeal, Paul's Plan
   d. Questions and Answers, The Harsh Letter
   e. Paul's Defense, Doctrine, Ethics

B. TEACHINGS: Circle the letter of the ONE BEST answer for each.

1. In legal disputes between Christians, Paul advised the victim to:
   a. Ask a fellow Christian to decide the issue.
   b. Have the aggressor put out of the fellowship.
   c. Point out the fault to his attacker.
   d. Accept the wrong rather than go before a pagan court.
   e. a and d

2. Christians know they are the sons of God, not slaves because:
   a. They are obedient.
   b. They receive the Spirit.
   c. Abraham is their ancestor.
   d. This was revealed to Paul.
   e. a and b

3. When the Corinthians questioned the raising from death of Christians Paul said:
   a. They would be raised as Christ had been.
   b. They had to wait a little longer.
   c. The Jews would return first.
   d. Many had been raised before that time.
   e. They should pray for greater faith.

4. Paul said a Christian could keep the whole Law by:
   a. Commitment and discipline
   b. Loving his fellowman
   c. Spending his life in deeds of service
   d. Participating in the Lord's Supper
   e. All of the above

5. Abraham was put right with God through faith:
   a. When Jesus was crucified
   b. For forty years
   c. And was accepted as righteous
   d. Upon being circumcised
   e. In fulfillment of the Law

6. The purpose of the Law was to:
   a. Put men right with God
   b. To be an instructor to men
   c. To keep Israel one
   d. To let men know they had sinned
   e. b and d

7. Concerning immorality, Paul told the Corinthians:
   a. If they turned to immorality they were no longer Christians.
   b. Marry to avoid it.
   c. The body belongs to God.
   d. God values love in all its forms.
   e. b and c

In each of the following groups, write the number of the partial teaching on the blank of the phrase which most nearly completes its meaning.

____No revenge
____Head covering for women
____Result of faith in Christ
____Gift of the Spirit
____The church
____Treasure in clay pots
____Love

1. Freedom from the Law
2. Power belongs to God.
3. Recognition of sonship
4. Eternal and happy with truth
5. Return good for evil.
6. Unity of Christ's body
7. Avoid disgrace.

____Concerning unbelievers
____The unseen
____Help received
____Freedom from Law
____All men
____Christ's death

1. Lasts forever
2. Not license but service
3. Sin
4. Don't work with them as equals.
5. Power and wisdom of God
6. To be passed on to others

C. FEATURES: Identify each of the following items as distinguishing features of each basic Letter by writing R, 1C, 2C, or G--for Romans, 1 Corinthians, 2 Corinthians, or Galatians--on each blank.

1. ____Written to a church Paul had never visited
2. ____Paul defends himself and affirms the gospel's freedom.
3. ____Written to reply to questions
4. ____Attempt to repair broken relations
5. ____Divisions and disorders
6. ____Sin brought by one man and freedom from sin by another
7. ____Hagar and Sarah
8. ____Paul agonizes and rejoices.
9. ____Faith, hope, and love
10. ____Effects of faith
11. ____Human nature (the flesh) versus the Spirit
12. ____The guilt of man
13. ____Nothing can separate us from God's love.
14. ____Probably not just one Letter
15. ____Grafting Gentiles into Jewish tree
16. ____Bearing burdens for each other
17. ____Speaking in tongues
18. ____Paul's reluctant display of credentials
19. ____Order and meaning in worship
20. ____Duty to the state
21. ____Christians are Abraham's spiritual descendants.
22. ____Paul's autobiography
23. ____Prisoners led in victory procession
24. ____Rejection by Jews resulted in salvation for Gentiles.
25. ____The way of love

Check your answers, and compute your score on page 8.

ANSWERS TO PRE-TEST FOR UNIT 1

A. STRUCTURE (5)   B. TEACHINGS (20)

1. a   1. e   5   4
2. d   2. b   7   1
3. d   3. a   1   6
4. c   4. b   3   2
5. e   5. c   6   3
                          6. e   2   5
                          7. e   4

C. FEATURES (25)

1. R   9. 1C   17. 1C
2. G   10. R   18. 2C
3. 1C   11. G   19. 1C
4. 2C   12. R   20. R
5. 1C   13. R   21. R or G
6. R   14. 2C   22. G
7. G   15. R   23. 2C
8. 2C   16. G   24. R
                              25. 1C

PRE-TEST SCORES FOR UNIT 1

Write the number correct for each category in the number column. Then compute the score according to the directions.

Category	# Correct	% Score	Directions
A. Structure	____ = ____		# Correct times 20 = %
B. Teachings	____ = ____		# Correct times 5 = %
C. Features	____ = ____		# Correct times 4 = %
Total (A+B+C)	____ = ____		# times 2 = %

Now record your scores on the Unit Growth Record on page 49. Then you will be ready to begin the study on Unit 1 on the next page.

UNIT 1: THE BASIC LETTERS

The first four Letters in the New Testament, the Basic Letters, have been included in the same unit because they share several characteristics. The canonical order demonstrates that this was understood by the early church.

1. They were all unquestionably written by Paul.
2. They all express essentials of Paul's basic theology.
3. They are the four longest Pauline epistles.

The four Letters were also written fairly close in time, during the period A.D. 52-56, unless Galatians was written earlier as some believe.

Of the four Letters, Romans, though the latest, is the most basic. Since it was written to introduce Paul and his theology to the Roman church before he visited them, it concentrates on theological position rather than on attempts to solve problems in a local church as do his Letters to Corinthians and Galatians. It is also the most formal Letter.

Although we cannot be sure what structure Paul had in mind, we are asking you to learn certain major divisions in each Letter. This will help you remember the content and also enable you to locate specific passages more easily.

To help you learn this structure, the major outline headings are presented within the structure of a building or column. The first heading is the bottom portion of the building; the next headings are the different levels of the building; and the conclusion or last part is the top. The complete building for each Letter or column appears without labels on this page. As you read the Letter, you will "build the edifice." An assignment to read the passages under the first heading will be accompanied by a picture of the first level of the structure with the balance of it in dotted lines. Each new outline heading will add to the construction.

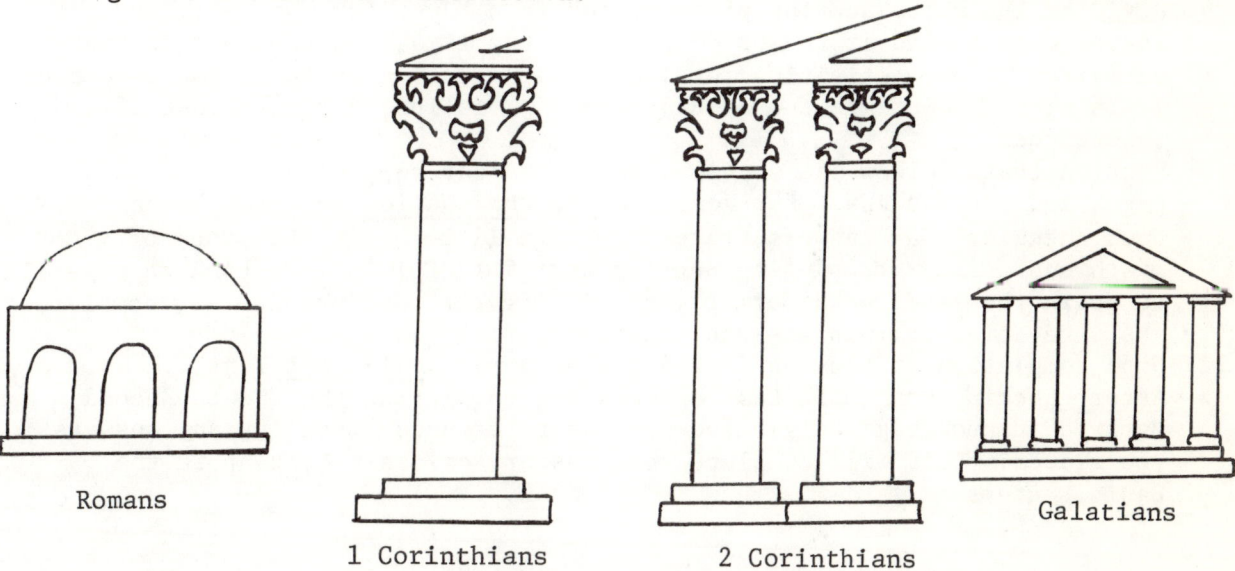

Romans 1 Corinthians 2 Corinthians Galatians

INSTRUCTIONS

The questions which guide your reading of the New Testament have been written on divided pages, so that you do not read down a page, but turn a page after reading only one divided portion. This probably seems strange to you, and at first it may be awkward. However you will soon find it very helpful. After thinking of your answers to the two or three questions, you turn the page to see the answers. If the questions went straight down the page, you would have to keep turning back and forth because you could not remember so many answers at one time.

In Unit 1, the Basic Letters, the questions and answers which guide the reading of Romans appear on the top quarter of each page, numbered in the 10's. Those which guide the reading of First and Second Corinthians appear on the second and third quarters, numbered in the 20's and 30's. The questions which guide the reading of Galatians appear on the bottom quarter page and are numbered in the 40's. You will read ONE BOOK at a time.

A reading assignment is given for each outline heading. To proceed:

1. <u>Note outline heading</u>.
2. <u>Read the questions</u> about one book on one page to guide your reading.
3. <u>Read the Bible passage</u> assigned.
4. <u>Reread the questions</u> and then <u>try to answer</u> them from memory. (You need not write the answers unless this helps you.)
5. <u>Look at the Bible</u> to finish answering the questions.
6. Then and ONLY THEN <u>turn the page to check</u> your answers.
7. Note the drawings; they will help you remember the important points.
8. Periodically you will be referred to section charts which follow the divided pages. These section charts will add to your understanding of each book's structure (vertical), themes (horizontal), and features throughout. <u>Fill in blanks on the charts</u> covering the reading you have just completed. Correct your answers and <u>study that portion</u> of the chart before returning to the divided page section.
9. Dividing the major section of each book is a "Just for Fun" activity. If you do not find it fun or do not have the time, you need not do the activity. These activities involve the application of facts you have been learning and sometimes the acquisition of more information by use of references.
10. Section tests follow the section charts. After completing the divided pages and section chart for Romans, <u>take the section test</u> for Romans. Upon checking your answers, return to page 11 to begin the study of 1 Corinthians. After completing Section Test 2 (1 Cor.), turn back to page 11 to begin the study of 2 Corinthians. Using the same procedures, complete the study of 2 Corinthians and Galatians.
11. Upon completion of Section Test 4 (Galatians), <u>begin Unit Test 1</u>.
12. After checking your unit test answers and completing the Growth Record (growth in knowledge only), look up the references listed by any answers you missed. This will complete your mastery of basic content in the Basic Letters.

10 BACKGROUND OF ROMANS

AUTHOR AND DATE: Paul (Saul) of Tarsus, undoubted; probably A.D. 55-56 after stay in Ephesus and before trip to Jerusalem

READERS: Church in Rome which Paul did not found and had never visited

CIRCUMSTANCES: A congregation that included both Jewish and Gentile Christians

PURPOSE: To introduce himself and his message to the church in Rome and to gain their support for his mission to Spain. (Turn to next page.)

20 BACKGROUND OF FIRST CORINTHIANS

AUTHOR: Paul, undoubted

DATE AND PLACE OF WRITING: From Ephesus where Paul stayed A.D. 52-55

READERS: Church in Corinth which Paul had founded about A.D. 49-50, and to which he had already written a letter now lost

PURPOSE: To settle disputes in the Corinthian church (Gnostics?), answer questions in a letter they had written, and advise them on other problems Paul had heard about. (Turn to next page.)

****

30 BACKGROUND OF SECOND CORINTHIANS

AUTHOR: Paul, undoubted

DATE AND PLACE: A.D. 55 from Ephesus near end of stay, and soon afterward from Macedonia

READERS: Church in Corinth

NATURE: Probably composed of two to five letters or parts of letters from Paul to Corinth

CIRCUMSTANCES AND PURPOSE: The church first rejected Paul's advice offered in First Corinthians; then Paul, by letters, by a personal visit, and by sending Titus, tried successfully to restore the broken relationship. (Turn to next page.)

****

40 BACKGROUND OF GALATIANS

AUTHOR: Paul, undoubted

READERS: Paul's Gentile converts in:
Region of Galatia (north)   or Province of Galatia (south)
about A.D. 53-55   about A.D. 49 or 53-55

CIRCUMSTANCES: Argument about whether or not Christians must be circumcised and keep the Jewish Law

10 BACKGROUND OF ROMANS

1. Romans was written by _____ about A.D. _____.

2. It was written to (or to do) ALL of the following EXCEPT:
   a. The church in Rome
   b. A church recently established by Paul
   c. A church of Gentiles with some Jews
   d. To introduce Paul
   e. To gain their support for his mission to Spain

Check previous page for answers, and proceed.

****

20 BACKGROUND OF FIRST CORINTHIANS

1. First Corinthians was written by _____.

2. It was written around:
   a. A.D. 43-47
   b. A.D. 52-55
   c. A.D. 58-59
   d. A.D. 62-65
   e. A.D. 76-79

3. Paul wrote the Letter:
   a. Because he was going there
   b. To settle disputes
   c. To answer questions
   d. To counteract Apollos' influence
   e. b and c

Check previous page for answers, and then proceed.

****

30 BACKGROUND OF SECOND CORINTHIANS

1. Written by _____ in A.D. _____ from _____ and _____

2. Second Corinthians is different from most of Paul's Letters in that:
   a. Paul had never been there.
   b. It was probably written by a later Christian.
   c. It is probably two or more letters.
   d. Paul uses a different style.

3. Paul tried to restore the relationship by ALL of the following methods EXCEPT:
   a. Recognizing the new leaders
   b. Writing letters
   c. Sending Titus to them
   d. Visiting them himself

Check previous page for answers, and then proceed.

****

40 BACKGROUND OF GALATIANS

1. Galatians was written by _____ ca. _____ or _____.

2. Readers were:
   a. Paul's Gentile converts
   b. Christians obeying the Law
   c. From region of Galatia
   d. From Province of Galatia
   e. a and (c or d)

3. Paul tried to counteract trouble:
   a. Caused by Apollos' teaching
   b. With Roman authorities
   c. About circumcision and the Law
   d. From a misunderstood letter
   e. With Jews or Greek unbelievers

Check previous page for answers.

11 OPENING: PLANS TO VISIT: 1:1-15

12 DOCTRINE: 1:16--11:35

12A Put Right with God (Justified)
    Through Faith: 1:16--8:39
    Read: Romans 1:1--3:20

   In 1:16 Paul states his theme:
   God puts men right with himself.

1. What is wrong with man?
2. What does the Law make men know
   about themselves?

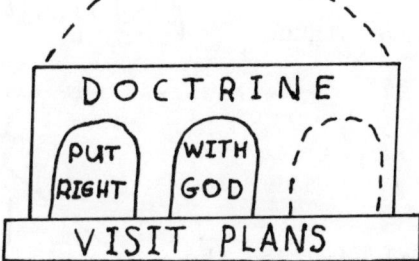

(Turn to the next page.)

****

21 OPENING: 1:1-9

22 DISORDERS IN CORINTH: 1--6

22A Factions. Read: 1 Cor. 1--4

  1. What disturbing news had Chloe's
     family reported?

(Turn to the next page.)

****

31 OPENING: 1:1-11
    Read: 2 Cor. 1:1--2:13

   Why does Paul say God helps
   Christians in trouble?

32 CHANGE IN TRAVEL PLANS: 1:12--2:13

   Why did Paul change his original plan to
   visit Corinth? (This passage is concluded in 7:5-16.)

(Turn to the next page.)

****

41 OPENING: 1-15

42 PAUL'S DEFENSE: APOSTLESHIP
    AND GOSPEL. Read: Gal.1--2

42A Paul's Charge Against the
    Galatians: 1:6-9

   What does Paul say the Galatians
   were doing?

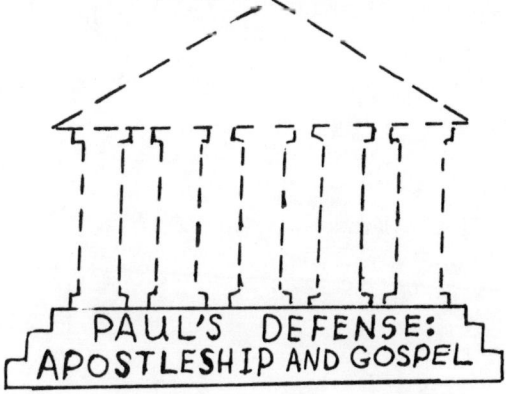

12A

1. He sins.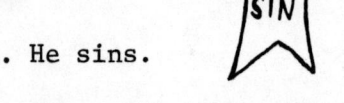

2. That they have sinned

****

22A

1. Arguments had divided the church into four factions.

****

31

So they can help others using the help they have been given

32

He wanted to spare the Corinthians. (If he had come they would have made each other sad.)

****

42A

The Galatians were deserting him and going to another gospel.

12A Put Right with God Through Faith
    Read: Romans 3:21--4:25

3. How will all men be put right with God?

4. Why was Abraham accepted as righteous?

5. Who are the spiritual descendants of Abraham?

　　　　　　*************************************

22A Factions

2. Paul emphasized the message of Christ's death in answering them. What did some Corinthians value that Paul rejected as a way of knowing God?

3. While Christ on the cross may be offensive to the Jews and nonsense to the Gentiles, what is it to believers?

　　　　　　***************************

33   PAUL'S MESSAGE AND MISSION: 2:14--6:13

33A Prisoners in Christ's Victory Procession
     READ: 2 Cor. 2:14--4:15

   What relationship makes Christians prisoners led by God in victory?

　　　　　　***************************

42B Autobiographical Section: 1:10--2:10

1. What had been revealed to Paul?

2. What did the church leaders at Jerusalem understand as the tasks given to Peter and to Paul?

12A

3. Through their faith in Jesus Christ
   (By the free gift of God's grace through Jesus Christ)

4. Because he had faith in God

5. All who believe in God and are accepted as righteous by him

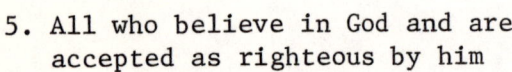

22A

2. Human knowledge and wisdom

3. The power and wisdom of God

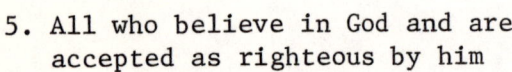

33A

Being in union with Christ

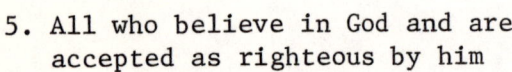

42B

1. The gospel of Christ

2. Peter's mission was to preach to the Jews, and Paul's, to preach to the Gentiles.

12A Put Right with God Through Faith
   READ: Romans 5--8

6. The effects of faith are described in these chapters. When a person has been put right with God, what is the first thing he will receive?

7. Through one man, sin came into the world; and through one man, freedom from sin was given. Who are these two men?

8. What is the relationship of the Christian to the Law? Why?

   ****

22B Sexual Immorality and Litigation
   READ: 1 Corinthians 5--6

1. When a Christian has a legal complaint against a fellow Christian, what is he told to do?

2. Why must a Christian avoid immorality--the sin against his own body?

   ****

33B Letter and Spirit; Law and Freedom: 3

   What does Paul say brings death? What brings life?

33C Treasure in Clay Pots (Earthen Vessels): 4:1-15

   Why does Paul say that Christians are like clay pots holding treasure?

   ****

42C Put Right with God Through Faith: 2:11-21

   What does Paul say it would mean if a man could be put right with God through the Law?

12A

6. The peace of God

7. Adam and Christ

8. The Christian is free from the Law because he is dead to sin and alive to God.

****

22B

1. He is told to have a fellow Christian decide the dispute or allow himself to be wronged rather than to go to a heathen court.

2. The Spirit lives in the Christian's body, and the Christian belongs to God, not to himself.

****

33B

The written Law brings death. The Spirit brings life.

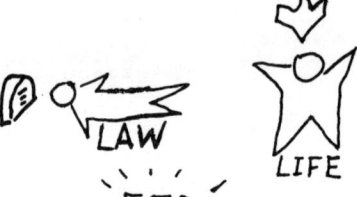

33C

To show that supreme power belongs to God, not to themselves

****

42C

It would mean that Christ died for nothing.

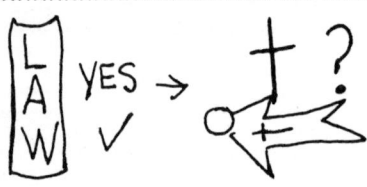

Now turn to page 36 to fill in blanks 1-5 on Section Chart 4. Check your answers on page 37. Study the corrected chart, and continue work on page 19.

12A Put Right with God Through Faith

9. What does living according to the Spirit enable people to become? (ch. 8)

10. What does God do for those who love him?

11. What does Paul say about separation of the Christian from God's love?

****

23 ANSWERS TO QUESTIONS FROM CORINTH.   READ: 1 Cor. 7--10

23A Celibacy and Marriage: 7

Paul's advice to remain single was probably based upon his expectation of Christ's return at any moment. Why then does he suggest marriage for the Corinthians?

23B Food Offered to Idols: 8--10

Why does Paul say a Christian should restrict himself in front of those who consider it wrong to eat certain foods?

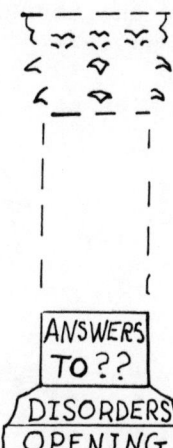

****

33D What Ends; What Lasts: 4:16--5:10
    READ: 2 Corinthians 4:16--6:13

To what should Christians give their attention and why?

33E Reconciliation Through Christ; All Things New: 5:11--6:2

What happens when a person is joined to Christ?

****

43 DOCTRINE: LAW OR FAITH
   READ: Galatians 3--4

43A Priority of Faith: 3:1-9

How was Abraham made righteous before God?

19

12A

9. Sons or children of God

10. "In all things God works for good with those who love him." (8:28)

11. Nothing can ever separate us from the love of God (8:38-39).

Turn now to page 33 to complete blanks 1-5 on Section Chart 1. Check your answers on page 37. Study the corrected chart, and then turn back to page 21 to continue Section 1.

****

23A

Because of their immorality

23B

Because something is sinful if a person thinks it is, and a Christian should not cause the weak man to sin

Now turn to page 34 to fill in blanks 1-5 on Section Chart 2. Check your answers on page 37. Study the corrected chart, and then continue work on page 21.

****

33D

To things which are unseen because they last forever

33E

He becomes a new being.

****

43A

Through faith

JUST FOR FUN!

See if you can find ten or more of the 18 key words from Romans in this word grid. They may be vertical, horizontal, or diagonal ... forwards or backwards!

Draw around each one you find. They are listed according to direction on the next page.

```
T S I R H C E Y E
S G O M J W V T S
G U R N E F I L I
H R O M W A L I M
H E A E S I N U O
T D L C T T B G R
A C K L E H B U P
E L I T N E G O D
D L E P S O G I Z
S P I R I T Y F R
```

****

24   CONCERNING WORSHIP: 11--14

24A Head Covering for Women
     READ: 1 Cor. 11

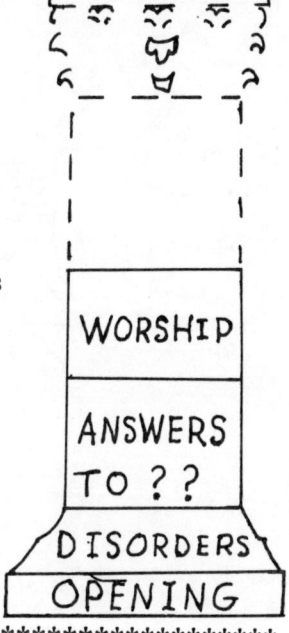

Paul says that it was the custom in the churches of God for women to cover their heads in public worship. What three reasons does Paul give?

24B The Lord's Supper

Paul says that the Corinthian meetings were harmful because they didn't come to eat the Lord's Supper. What did they do? What did they sin against?

****

33F A Personal Appeal: 6:3-13

Paul says he has been frank with the Corinthians, but they have been closed to him. What does he ask them to show him?

(This passage may be concluded in 7:2-4.)

****

43B Law Versus Promise: 3:10-18

God's promise was to Abraham and his descendant, Christ. Who does Paul say are Abraham's true descendants?

JUST FOR FUN!

Diagonal	Vertical	Horizontal
Righteous (B)	Jews	Gentile (B)
Grace	Live (B)	Sin
Adam	Faith	Life (B)
Son	Death (B)	Christ (B)
	Promise (B)	Spirit
	Guilt (B)	Gospel (B)
		Law (B)
		God

Note: (B) = backwards.

****

24A

Reasons:

1. An uncovered head is the equivalent of the shameful shaved head.
2. A covered head shows that a wife is under her husband's authority.
3. Nature teaches that long hair is a woman's pride.

24B

Each went ahead with his own meal so that some were hungry and some got drunk. They were sinning against the Lord's body and blood.

****

33F

The same feelings which he has for them

****

43B

All who believe in Christ

12B Problem: The Promise to Israel
READ: Romans 9--11

1. Paul describes the choosing (election) of Israel. When God told Abraham, "Only the descendants of Isaac shall be counted as yours," whom did God identify as children of God?

2. Why were the Gentiles put right with God when they did not try?

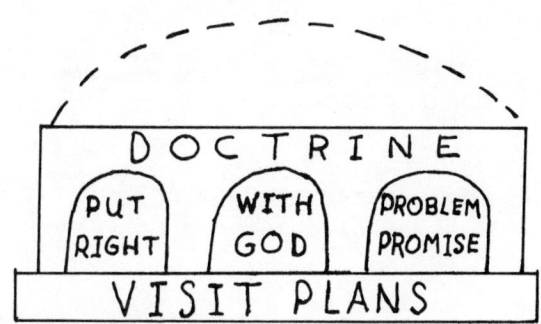

****

JUST FOR FUN!   The Lord's Supper at Corinth

Christians in Corinth disagreed about what was appropriate in worship. Just imagine what went on in the church service at Corinth which Paul describes in 1 Cor. 11:17-34. Consider:

1. Early Christians usually met in one member's home.
2. The people of Corinth were known for their wild and immoral living.
3. Most of the Corinthian Christians were Gentiles who had recently left the worship of idols, mystery cults, and fertility rites.
4. In the early years of Christianity, the celebration of the Lord's Supper was combined with a regular meal.

(Continued on the next page.)

****

JUST FOR FUN!

Second Corinthians does not tell about a journey, but the geographical references in it show that Paul was traveling as he wrote. The map on page 56 shows all the places Paul mentions in 2 Cor. 1--6. Write under each place the verse(s) in which that place is mentioned.

Try to reconstruct Paul's movements and to decide from what place he must have been writing.

****

JUST FOR FUN!   Paul's Autobiography

Galatians contains the best autobiography we have of Paul. He gives time intervals and places for the events he describes. See what you can learn about him. Refer to a map. (Acts 4 will help if you have Book II of the series.) Set up a table something like the one on the next page and fill it in.

23

12B

1. Children born as a result of
   God's promise

2. Because they had faith
   instead of depending on
   works

****

JUST FOR FUN!

Now imagine the scene when Paul's Letter is read to the church in Corinth. In the group are the person who had reported to Paul the disgraceful behavior (as he saw it) of some at the Lord's Supper and another person who really enjoyed those church suppers with good Greek wine. Imagine their conversation after hearing what Paul wrote. (If you are working alone, you might talk it through out loud.)

****

JUST FOR FUN!

At least two kinds of spoonerisms came from Oxford over a century ago. One is the transposition of initial consonants. Ex. "Live me giberty or give de meath." This you will recognize as "Give me liberty or give me death." Try these from 2 Corinthians:

1. The ditten wraw brings leath, but the lirit brings spife. (3:6b)

2. We reem to have sothing, yet we neally possess everything. (6:10b)

3. The san who mants few pleeds will have a crall smop. (9:6)

Another type transposes words or syllables. From 1 Cor. 11:10--A woman shall have a head over her husband to show that he is undercovering her authority.

****

JUST FOR FUN!   Paul's Autobiography

Time	Event	Persons	Places
1.	Saul persecutes Christians.		
2.	God reveals Son to Saul.		Damascus
3 years			
3.	To get information	Saul Peter James	

(Add preaching, report to apostles, and confrontation with Peter.)

12B   Problem: The Promise to Israel

3. Paul says the sin of the Jews resulted in salvation for the Gentiles. When Paul speaks of the grafting in of the Gentiles, why does he say they must not despise the Jews?

4. When will the Jews return to God according to Paul?

****

24C   Spiritual Gifts: 12--14
      READ: 1 Cor. 12--13

1. When Paul speaks of the unity of the single body of Christ and of the equal value and interdependence of its parts, to what single body and its parts is he referring?

2. Paul describes love as eternal and happy with truth. In what two other positive ways does he describe it?

3. Paul concludes chapter 13 by listing what have come to be known as the three Christian virtues. What are they, and which is the greatest?

****

34   A CALL TO SEPARATION AND PURITY
      READ: 2 Corinthians 6:14--7:1

   This passage is from Paul's lost letter. Others say it may be the work of another writer.

1. What guidance was given the Corinthians about allowing unbelievers in the Christian community?

35   PERSONAL APPEAL FOR ACCEPTANCE
      READ: 2 Corinthians 7:2-4

   This passage perhaps continues the text from 6:13. Paul repeats his request. What is it?

****

43C   Purpose of the Law: 3:19-29

   Until Christ came, what role did the Law play?

43D   Slaves or Sons: 4:1-11

   How did God show the Galatians that they were his sons?

12B

3. Because the Jewish root supports the Gentile branch

4. When the complete number of Gentiles come to God

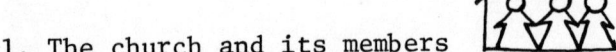

****

24C

1. The church and its members

2. Patient and kind

3. Faith, hope, and love
   Love is the greatest.

****

34

1. Not to try to work with them as equals, but to "leave them and separate yourselves from them." (6:17)

35

"Make room for us in your hearts." (7:2) (Compare with 6:13.)

****

43C

The role of instructor

43D

He sent the Spirit of his Son into their hearts.

13 EXHORTATION: ETHICS: 12:1--15:13

13A GENERAL PRINCIPLES. READ: Romans 12

1. How does God transform the believer?

2. Paul describes principles of conduct such as humility, sincerity, love. What does he say about revenge? (Compare Matt. 5:38-42.)

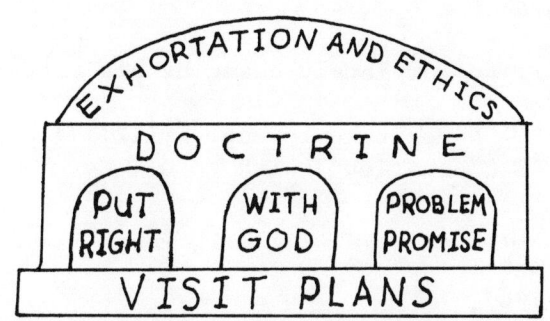

****

24C Spiritual Gifts: 12--14
    READ: 1 Corinthians 14

4. Evidently the Corinthians were fond of speaking in strange sounds during their worship. What does Paul say is better and why?

5. What two things does Paul emphasize in public worship?

****

36 CONFIDENCE RESTORED
    READ: 2 Corinthians 7:5-16

This passage may continue the text from 2:13.

Why was Paul encouraged by Titus message?

37 THE OFFERING FOR JERUSALEM
    READ: 2 Corinthians 8--9

Chapter 9 may be a separate letter on the same subject. What pleased Paul about the churches in Macedonia?

****

43E Personal Appeal: Follow Me! 4:12-20

Instead of turning back to the pitiful ruling spirits, what did Paul want the Galatians to do?

43F Allegory of Hagar and Sarah: 4:21-31

Sarah's son was born as the result of God's promise. What did the son of the slave woman do to him?

13A

1. By completely changing his mind

2. "Never take revenge." (12:19)
   Conquer evil with good.

****

24C

4. Speaking God's message so that one helps others

5. Order and meaning
   (to help each other)

****

36

Because Titus reported support of the Corinthians for Paul
(Compare 2:12-13 and 7:5-6.)

37

Even though poor, they gave very generously to the Judean Christians.

Now turn to page 35 to fill in blanks 1-6 on Section Chart 3. Check your answers on page 37. Study the corrected chart, and then continue work on page 29.

****

43E

He wanted them to follow him.

43F

Hagar's son persecuted Sarah's son.

Now turn to page 36 to fill in blanks 6-8 on Section Chart 4. Check your answers on page 37. Study the corrected chart, and then turn back to page 29 to finish Section 4.

13B Duty to the State: 13:1-7
     READ: Romans 13

   Why does Paul say the Roman Christians should obey state laws and pay taxes?

13C Duties to One Another: 13:8-14

   How can a Christian obey the whole Law?

   ****

25   RESURRECTION OF THE DEAD. READ: 1 Corinthians 15

1. Paul mentions six appearances by the resurrected Christ, including appearances to the Twelve, the 500, and to all the apostles again. What were the others?

2. How does Paul answer the Corinthian position that the dead will not be raised to life?

26   PAUL'S PLANS. READ: 1 Corinthians 16

26A The Offering for Jerusalem: 16:1-4

   How did Paul instruct the Corinthians to raise money for the poor Jewish Christians in Jerusalem?

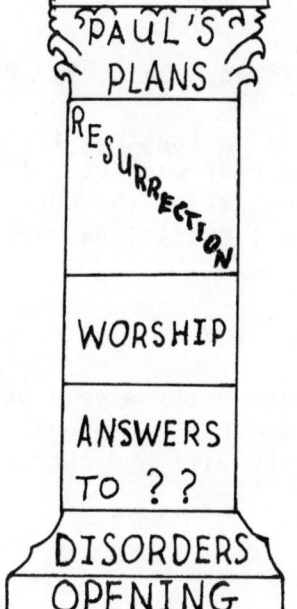

   ****

38   THE HARSH LETTER: 10--13
     READ: 2 Corinthians 10:1--11:15

38A Introduction: 10:1-6

38B Defense Against Accusations: 10:7--11:15

   How did Paul defend himself against the charge of preaching for money (worldly motives)?

   ****

44   ETHICS: FREEDOM AND SPIRIT. READ: Gal. 5--6

44A Freedom Versus Circumcision: 5:1-12

   Those who asked for circumcision put themselves outside God's grace for wanting to use their own power. What should the Christian seek and practice?

13B

Because existing authority comes from God

13C

By loving his neighbor

****

25

1. Peter, James, and Paul

2. By saying that if this were so, Christ was not raised from the dead, and the Corinthians (and all Christians) are still lost

26A

Each set aside a portion of his earnings so that Paul could send some members with the gift and letters to Jerusalem.

****

38B

He says he did not charge the Corinthians a thing while he preached the Good News to them.

****

44A

Faith that works through love

13D Mutual Acceptance: 14--15:12
     READ: Romans 14--15

1. The strong are to help the weak. What is it that both must refrain from doing?
2. What two groups should accept each other? (Both are mentioned in the Old Testament reference.)

13E Blessing: 15:13

14   CLOSING: 15:14-33

1. What did Paul consider his mission to be?
2. What was Paul's plan to visit Rome?

15   APPENDIX: 16
     (Some think these greetings belong with the Ephesian Letter.)
     ****

26B Travel Plans: 16:5-12

     What were the plans?

27   CLOSING: 16:13-24
     ****

38C Reluctant Display of Credentials: 11:16--12:13
     READ: 2 Corinthians 11:16--12:13

1. Paul says he has better credentials than false apostles and is a better servant. What had he undergone to make him better?
2. What is the reason Paul gives for his physical affliction?

38D Projected Third Visit: 12:14--13:10

     Why does Paul say he has written?

39   CLOSING: 13:11-13
     ****

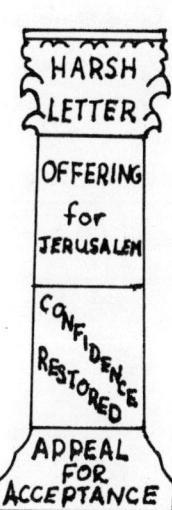

44B Living by the Spirit: 5:13--6:10

1. Paul warns against using freedom as an excuse. What does he advise?
2. Paul lists what human nature does (works of flesh). What does he then list in contrast?
3. What did Paul ask the Galatians to do for each other?

45   CLOSING: 6:11-18

     What was so important that Paul added a note in his own hand?

13D

1. Judging one another

2. Jews and Gentiles ("Rejoice, Gentiles, with God's chosen people!" --15:10)

14

1. Preaching to the Gentiles in places where Christ was not known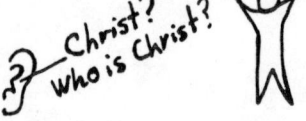

2. After taking the Gentile offering to the Jerusalem Christians, he would go to Rome on the way to Spain.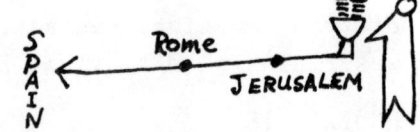

Complete the chart on p. 33. Check answers; review; take Sect. Test 1, p. 38.
****

26B

Paul was going to Macedonia and then on to Corinth where he would stay all winter.

Complete chart p. 34; take test p. 40.
****

38C

1. He had been imprisoned, near death several times, and whipped.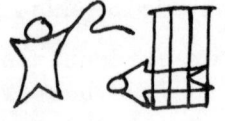

2. It was to keep him from being proud of his wonderful vision.

38D

So he won't have to deal harshly with them when he sees them.

Complete the chart on p. 35. Check answers; review; take Sect. Test 3, p. 41.
****

44B

1. To let love make Christians serve one another
2. Products (fruits) of the Spirit
3. Help carry one another's burdens.

45

The question of circumcision

Complete the chart on p. 36. Check answers; review; take Sect. Test 4, p. 43.

SECTION CHART 1: ROMANS
OPENING: PLANS TO VISIT

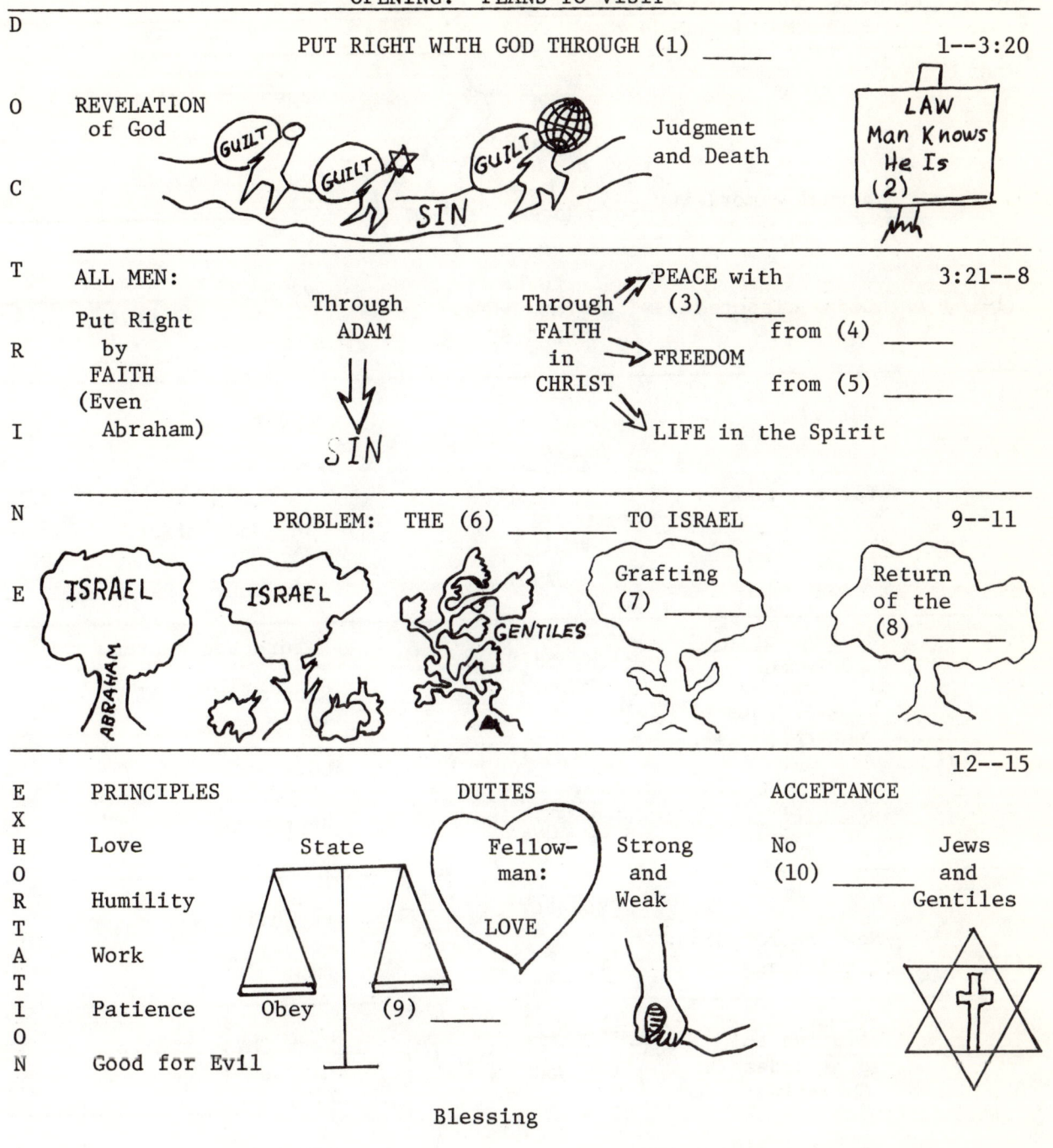

CLOSING

APPENDIX

Check answers on page 37, and study the corrected chart.

SECTION CHART 2: FIRST CORINTHIANS

Note: Problems and Answers columns apply to all chapters.

(Ch.)	PROBLEMS OF CHURCH		PAUL'S ANSWERS
(1--6)	Factions Sexual immorality Legal disputes	DISORDERS? POWER through CHRIST	Cross of Christ is (1) _____ Body belongs to (2) _____ (3) _____ should judge
(7--10)	Marry? Eat all food?	? FAITH	Only to (4) _____ But don't offend (5) _____
(11--14)	Head covering for women Hungry/drunk at church meetings Speaking in tongues	WORSHIP? LOVE	Nature and custom Know meaning of (6) _____ LOVE Better to (7) _____
(15)	No life for dead Christians	RESURRECTION? (9) _____	If Christ was raised, (8) _____
(16)	Offering to poor Judean Christians Pastoral visits	PAUL'S PLANS	Each Christian to set aside (10) _____ Stay all winter

Check answers on page 37, and study the corrected chart.

SECTION CHART 3: SECOND CORINTHIANS

OPENING

LETTER OF

CHANGE IN (1) _____
    1:12--2:13
Reference to letter (lost)
    2:3

        CONFIDENCE RESTORED
            7:5-16
        Report by Titus

        PAUL'S MESSAGE AND MISSION
            2:14--6:2
Prisoners in (2) _____ procession
The Spirit gives life and freedom.

(3) _____ in clay pots
Unseen things last forever. All things new in (4) _____

PERSONAL (5) _____   OFFERING FOR (6) _____
  6:3-13, 7:2-4   ch. 8

RECONCILIATION

SEPARATION AND PURITY
of the Christian community
(Lost letter of 2:3?)
6:14--7:1

GENEROUS GIVING
ch. 9
(Separate letter?)

HARSH

INTRODUCTION 10:1-6

    Paul accused of
    worldly motives.

DEFENSE AGAINST ACCUSATIONS
    10:7--11:15

Corinthians accepted

(7) _____ apostles.

Paul: No charge for preaching

RELUCTANT DISPLAY OF

(8) _____
    11:16--12:13
    Hardships
    Vision

PLAN FOR (9) _____ VISIT
    12:14--13:10

LETTER

CLOSING
13:11-13

Check answers on page 37, and study the corrected chart.

35

SECTION CHART 4: GALATIANS

Read outline in horizontal bands and themes in vertical columns.

OPENING

APOSTLESHIP AND GOSPEL (1--2)

THE LAW

Charge against Galatians:
Leaving the (1) _____

Paul's persecution of
church

PAUL'S DEFENSE

THE SPIRIT

Paul's Autobiography

(2) _____ to Paul

Preaching assignments:
Peter: (3) _____
 Paul: (4) _____

Put right through (5) _____

DOCTRINE (3--4)

THE LAW

Law: Instructor before
(7) _____

Jesus

Slaves . . . or . . . (8) _____

Others taught Law and slavery.

Hagar . . . and . . . Sarah

FAITH

Abraham made righteous
through faith

God's (6) _____ to Abraham,
Christ, and so to Christians

Appeal to follow Paul

ETHICS (5--6)

THE LAW

Circumcision:
 Outside God's grace

HUMAN NATURE

Physical desires rule:
 Wrong deeds

THE SPIRIT

(9) _____ from Law:

Let love make you serve.

Products: love, joy, peace . . .

Carry each other's (10) _____

CLOSING

Check answers on page 37, and study the corrected chart.

ANSWERS TO SECTION CHARTS

1. <u>Romans</u>

1. Faith
2. Sinner (guilty)
3. God
4. Sin
5. Law
6. Promise
7. Gentiles
8. Jews
9. Pay
10. Judgment

2. <u>1 Corinthians</u>

1. Power of God
2. God
3. Fellow Christians
4. Prevent immorality
5. Another's conscience
6. Lord's Supper
7. Tell God's message
8. Christians will be
9. Hope
10. Money (proportion)

3. <u>2 Corinthians</u>

1. Travel Plans
2. Victory
3. Treasure
4. Christ
5. Appeal
6. Jerusalem
7. False
8. Credentials
9. Third

4. <u>Galatians</u>

1. Gospel
2. Revelation
3. Jews
4. Gentiles
5. Faith
6. Promise
7. Christ
8. Sons
9. Freedom
10. Burdens

Note: Get the <u>sense</u> of the answer; exact wording does not usually matter.

SECTION TEST 1: ROMANS

A. STRUCTURE: Fill in the blanks to complete the following outline of Romans.

Opening: Plans to Visit

I. (1) _____

   A. (2) _____

   B. Problem: (3) _____

II. (4) _____
   A. General Principles
   B. Duty to the State
   C. Duties to One Another
   D. (5) _____
   E. Blessing (Benediction)

Closing
Appendix

B. TEACHINGS: Circle the ONE BEST answer in each statement.

1. All those who have faith and live according to the Spirit of God will experience ALL of the following EXCEPT:
   a. The peace of God
   b. Joy
   c. Success
   d. Hope
   e. Love
2. Believers are free from:
   a. The high priests and the Pharisees
   b. Sin and the Law
   c. Disease and evil spirits
   d. Roman rule
   e. The demands of human nature
3. Paul says that all men:
   a. Know the Law
   b. Sin
   c. Are put right with God
   d. Live in the Spirit
   e. b and c
4. Paul calls Christians Abraham's descendants because:
   a. They are his spiritual descendants by faith in God.
   b. They obey the Law.
   c. Abraham, like Adam, is father of all.
   d. The promise to Abraham was based upon faith.
   e. a and d

5. The men by whom sin and freedom came into the world are respectively:
   a. Adam and Abraham
   b. Abraham and Jesus Christ
   c. Adam and Jesus Christ
   d. Paul and Jesus
   e. Abraham and David

6. Paul says that God works for good (in those who love him):
   a. To show others the evil of their ways
   b. Because they force him
   c. In the things men do which please God
   d. To win men's love
   e. In everything

7. In speaking of the separation of the Christian from God's love, Paul says:
   a. Nothing can do it.
   b. Only evil powers can cause separation.
   c. There is no danger so long as the Christian is obedient.
   d. Only God can cause the separation.
   e. b and c

Write the number of each of the following subjects or results of Paul's teachings (right) before the phrase with which it is most closely associated (left). Use each number ONCE except #1.

1. ___ God's transformation method		1. Faith in God (use twice)
2. ___ Major principles of conduct		2. Peace with God
3. ___ Existing authority from God		3. Pay taxes and obey law.
4. ___ Obey the whole Law.		4. Salvation for the Gentiles
5. ___ Men who are different		5. Love your neighbor.
6. ___ Scriptural prediction		6. Complete change of mind
7. ___ First gift to believer		7. Conquer by doing good.
8. ___ Jewish rejection of Christ		8. Love, humility, forgiveness
9. ___ Living according to the Spirit		9. Jews and Gentiles rejoice together.
10. ___ Purpose of the Law		10. Make men aware of their sin.
11. ___ What Abraham had		11. Enables people to become children of God
12. ___ Fighting evil		12. Refrain from judging each other.
13. ___ How Gentiles are put right with God		

Check your answers on page 45, and compute your scores below.

Write the number of items correct in the # column. Compute the % as directed, and write on the % column. Then enter your scores on the Unit 1 Growth Record on page 49.

Category	# Correct	% Score	Directions
A. Structure	___	= ___	# Correct times 20 = %
B. Teachings	___	= ___	# Correct times 5 = %
Total (A+B) (Maximum 25)	___	= ___	# Correct times 4 = %

SECTION TEST 2: FIRST CORINTHIANS

A. STRUCTURE: Fill in the blanks to complete the following outline.
    Opening
    I. (1) _____
        A. Factions
        B. Immorality and Litigation
    II. (2) _____
        A. Celibacy and Marriage
        B. Food Offered to Idols
    III. (3) _____
        A. Head Covering for Women
        B. The Lord's Supper
        C. Spiritual Gifts
    IV. (4) _____
    V. Paul's Plans
        A. Offering to Jerusalem
        B. Travel Plans

    Closing

B. TEACHINGS: Circle the letter of the ONE BEST answer to each.

1. Paul's answer to the factions in the Corinthian church was:
    a. Discussion and compromise
    b. Repentance and confession
    c. The power of Christ
    d. Obedience to the Law
    e. b and d

2. The meaning of Christ's death was ALL of the following EXCEPT:
    a. Wisdom to those being lost
    b. Offensive to the Jews
    c. Impossible to know through man's wisdom
    d. Nonsense to the Gentiles
    e. God's power to those being saved

3. Concerning worship, Paul discussed ALL of the following EXCEPT:
    a. Head covering for women
    b. The Lord's Supper
    c. The Lord's Prayer
    d. Faith, hope, and love
    e. Unity of Christ's body

4. Paul describes love as ALL of the following EXCEPT:
    a. Happy with truth
    b. Patient
    c. Kind
    d. Able to move mountains
    e. Eternal

40

The following chart lists problems and questions which the Corinthians brought to Paul and Paul's answers to them. Fill in the blanks to complete the list.

PROBLEMS	ANSWERS
(1) _____	Power through Christ
Immorality	(2) _____
(3) _____	Fellow Christian should judge.
Marriage	(4) _____
(5) _____	Don't offend another's conscience.
(6) _____	Nature and custom support it.
Speaking in tongues	(7) _____
No life for dead Christians	(8) _____

FEATURES: Circle the numbers of three features in First Corinthians which distinguish it from Romans.

1. Attempts to solve church problems
2. Adam and Christ
3. Faith, hope, and love
4. Chapter about resurrection
5. A church Paul had never visited
6. Nothing can separate us from God's love.

Check your answers on page 45, and compute your scores below. Then enter them on the Unit 1 Growth Record, page 49.

Category	# Correct	% Scores	Directions
A. Structure	____ = ____		# Correct times 20 = %
B. Teachings and Features	____ = ____		See chart below.
Total (A+B)	____ = ____		# times 5 = %

#	1	2	3	4	5	6	7	8	9	10	11	12	13	14	15	#
%	7	13	20	27	33	40	47	53	60	67	73	80	87	93	100	%

SECTION TEST 3: SECOND CORINTHIANS

A. STRUCTURE: Fill in the blanks to complete the outline.

    Opening
  I. Change in Travel Plans
 II. Paul's (1) _____
III. A Call to (2) _____
 IV. A Personal (3) _____
  V. (4) _____
 VI. Offering for Jerusalem
VII. The (5) _____
    Closing

B. TEACHINGS: Circle the letter of the ONE BEST answer to each.

1. Paul did not go to Corinth as planned because:
    a. He was needed in Ephesus.
    b. The Corinthians said he should not come.
    c. He would have misled them.
    d. He wanted to spare the Corinthians.
    e. He was ill.

2. When Paul told of his love for the Corinthians, he appealed to them to:
    a. Show this love toward all men.
    b. Give extra money to Jerusalem.
    c. Provide his living the next time he visited them
    d. Stop closing their minds toward him.
    e. Stop criticizing him.

3. Paul says that spiritual treasure was put in "clay pot" Christians:
    a. To help them
    b. Because God is gracious
    c. To emphasize that power belongs to God
    d. Because God treats all men alike
    e. b and d

4. Paul invites Christians to give their attention to unseen things rather than to visible ones because:
    a. They know visible things do not last.
    b. They want to be more spiritual.
    c. They have few worldly possessions.
    d. They know that unseen things last forever.
    e. a and d

5. Paul advised the Corinthians:
    a. That they should consider all men their equals
    b. That they should not work with unbelievers as equals
    c. To stop discriminating among men
    d. To separate themselves from unbelievers
    e. b and d

Write the number of each partial teaching on the blank before the phrase with which it is most closely associated.

____	Christians as prisoners	1.	Poor Macedonian churches
____	Person in union with Christ	2.	Preaching for money
____	Gave to Judean Christians	3.	Brings death; brings life
____	Paul accused of this	4.	Led in victory by God
____	Christians given help	5.	A new being
____	Repentant Corinthians	6.	Paul's credentials
____	Law; Spirit	7.	To pass it on to others
____	Hardships and vision	8.	Good report from Titus

FEATURES: Circle the numbers of two features which distinguish 2 Corinthians.

1. Problems and answers
2. May be parts of several letters
3. The promise to Israel
4. Paul agonizes and rejoices.
5. Obey and pay.
6. Speaking in tongues

Check your answers on page 45. Compute your scores below and then enter them on the Unit 1 Growth Record, page 49.

Category	# Correct	% Score	Directions
A. Structure	___	= ___	# Correct times 20 = %
B. Teachings	___	= ___	See chart for 15#, page 41
Total (A+B)	___	= ___	# Correct times 5

SECTION TEST 4: GALATIANS

A. STRUCTURE: Fill in the blanks of the following outline.

Opening

I. (1) _____ Apostleship and Gospel
    A. Paul's Charge Against the Galatians
    B. (2) _____
    C. Put Right with God Through Faith

II. (3) _____ : Law or Faith
    A. Priority of Faith
    B. (4) _____
    C. Purpose of Law
    D. Slaves or Sons
    E. Personal Appeal: Follow Me!
    F. Allegory of Hagar and Sarah

III. (5) _____ : Freedom and Spirit
    A. Freedom Versus Circumcision
    B. Living by the Spirit

Closing

B. TEACHINGS: Write the number of each partial teaching on the blank before the phrase with which it is most closely associated.

____ Galatians wanted this.
____ Products of Spirit versus
____ If Law justified men
____ Abraham
____ Abraham's descendants
____ Sons and not slaves

1. What human nature does
2. Made righteous by faith before circumcision
3. Another gospel
4. Those who believe in Christ
5. Christ died for nothing.
6. Gift of Spirit

Circle the letter of the ONE BEST answer for each statement.

1. Paul said he received the gospel he preached:
    a. Directly from Christ
    b. From talks with Peter
    c. From information given by James, Peter, and John
    d. From Barnabas and Titus
    e. From reading the Scriptures

2. The church leaders agreed that God had given Paul the task of:
    a. Traveling over the world
    b. Preaching to the Jews of the Dispersion
    c. Telling all men the story of Jesus' life
    d. Preaching the gospel to the Gentiles
    e. Baptizing the Gentiles

3. Until Christ came the purpose of the Law was:
    a. To put men right with God
    b. To teach men what wrongdoing was
    c. To keep men from receiving God's promise
    d. To make men God's sons
    e. a and d

4. The Christian who requested circumcision:
    a. Had to obey the entire Law
    b. Lost his freedom
    c. Was outside God's grace
    d. Was trying to substitute his power for God's
    e. All of above

C. FEATURES: Circle five numbers of items which distinguish Galatians.

1. Burden bearing
2. Clay pots
3. Food offered to idols
4. Hagar and Sarah
5. Autobiography
6. Attempt to restore relations
7. Problem of circumcision
8. Speaking in tongues
9. Grafting in the Gentiles
10. Faith that works through love

Check your answers on page 45, and compute your scores below.

Category	# Correct	% Score	Directions
A. Structure	____ = ____		# Correct times 20 = %
B. Teachings	____ = ____		# Correct times 10 = %
C. Features	____ = ____		# Correct times 20 = %
Total (A+B+C)	____ = ____		# Correct times 5 = %

Record your scores on the Unit 1 Growth Record on page 49.

Review the material for any category in which you made less than 90% on any section test. Then take the unit test, page 46.

ANSWERS TO SECTION TESTS

Section 1   STRUCTURE (5)

1. Doctrine
2. Put Right with God Through Faith
3. The Promise to Israel
4. Exhortation: Ethics (or just "Ethics")
5. Mutual Acceptance

TEACHINGS (20)

1. c	1. 6	8. 4
2. b	2. 8	9. 11
3. b	3. 3	10. 10
4. e	4. 5	11. 1
5. c	5. 12	12. 7
6. e	6. 9	13. 1
7. a	7. 2	

Section 2   STRUCTURE (5)

1. Disorders
2. Answers to Questions
3. Worship
4. Resurrection
5. Paul's Plans

1. c
2. a
3. c
4. d

TEACHINGS AND FEATURES (15)

1. Divisions	1
2. Body belongs to God.	3
3. Legal disputes	4
4. To prevent immorality	
5. Food offered to idols.	
6. Head covering	
7. Better to tell God's message	
8. If Christ was raised, all will rise.	

Section 3   STRUCTURE (5)

1. Mission and Message
2. Separation and Purity
3. Appeal
4. Confidence
5. Harsh Letter

1. d
2. d
3. c
4. e
5. e

TEACHINGS AND FEATURES (15)

4	2
5	4
1	
2	
7	
8	
3	
6	

Section 4   STRUCTURE (5)

1. Paul's Defense
2. Autobiography
3. Doctrine
4. Law Versus Promise
5. Ethics

3
1
5
2
4
6

TEACHINGS (10)

1. a
2. d
3. b
4. e

FEATURES (5)

1
4
5
7
10

UNIT TEST 1: BASIC LETTERS

A. STRUCTURE: Fill in the blanks of the following outlines.

Romans
    I. (1) _____
        A. (2) _____
        B. Problem: (3) _____
    II. (4) _____

1 Corinthians
    I. (5) _____
    II. (6) _____ to _____
    III. (7) _____
    IV. (8) _____
    V. Paul's (9) _____

2 Corinthians
    I. Change in Travel Plans
    II. (10) _____
    III. A Call to (11) _____
    IV. Personal Appeal
    V. (12) _____ of _____
    VI. (13) _____ for Jerusalem
    VII. (14) _____

Galatians
    I. (15) _____
    II. (16) _____
    III. (17) _____

B. TEACHINGS: Circle the letter of the ONE BEST answer to each.

1. Christians were made prisoners led by God in victory:
    a. In union with Christ
    b. Because of their sin
    c. To make Christ known to all men
    d. Through their good deeds
    e. a and c

2. ALL of the following were identified as brought by the Spirit EXCEPT:
    a. Knowledge that man has sinned
    b. Freedom from sin
    c. Life
    d. Peace
    e. Freedom from death

3. When a fellow Christian wronged a man, the victim was told it was better to:
    a. Be wronged than to go to the heathen court
    b. Point out the fault than to suffer in silence
    c. Take legal action than to condone the wrong
    d. Have the sinner put outside the fellowship than to let him corrupt it
    e. c and d

4. In corporate worship Paul stressed the need for ALL of the following EXCEPT:
   a. Order
   b. Giving message
   c. Speaking in tongues
   d. Head covering for women
   e. Knowing meaning of Lord's body

5. Paul told of Hagar and Sarah as an allegory which concerned:
   a. The relationship of men to God
   b. Christians and unbelievers
   c. Men as slaves or sons of God
   d. Christ and the spirits of evil
   e. a, b, and c

6. The Jews had erred in relying on the Law to put them right with God because:
   a. The Law has nothing to do with God.
   b. They ignored the Gentiles.
   c. They depended on works.
   d. They didn't keep the Law.
   e. c and d

7. Paul teaches that the Jews will believe the Good News and be saved:
   a. After they have all been punished
   b. When they keep the complete Law
   c. When the full number of Gentiles believes
   d. As they adopt Gentile ways
   e. When their nation is fully restored

8. When the Corinthians said Christians would not rise from death Paul said that:
   a. Then Christ died for nothing.
   b. Then they were lost.
   c. If Christ was raised, all Christians would be, too.
   d. Then they had no hope.
   e. All of the above

9. All of the following were given as products of the Spirit (fruits of the Spirit) EXCEPT:
   a. Suffering
   b. Self-control
   c. Patience
   d. Humility
   e. Faithfulness

10. Titus brought Paul news of:
    a. The divisions in the church at Corinth
    b. The Corinthians' support of Paul
    c. The decision to give to Jerusalem
    d. The many new converts
    e. Immorality at Corinth

For each of the following groups, write the number of EACH partial teaching on the blank before the ONE phrase with which it is most closely associated.

___ Fulfilled Law by
___ All men
___ Compared with Christ
___ Faith in Christ
___ Descendants of Abraham
___ Purpose of Law
___ Fight evil with

1. Adam
2. Men know they sinned.
3. Put right by faith
4. Children born of God's promise
5. Good
6. Love for neighbor
7. Freedom from Law

___ Avoid immorality
___ Head covering for women
___ Marriage
___ At Lord's Supper
___ Speaking in tongues
___ If Christ raised
___ Concerning unbelievers

1. To avoid shame and by custom
2. Better to tell God's message
3. To avoid immorality
4. Body belongs to God.
5. All Christians will be resurrected.
6. Don't work with them as equals.
7. Know the meaning of the Lord's body.

___ Abraham before circumcision
___ Unseen things
___ Christians given help
___ Law and Spirit
___ Paul's charge against Galatians
___ Burdens
___ The Law
___ Alternate to license
___ Revealed Christ

1. Death and life
2. God, in his grace to Paul
3. Faith that works through love
4. Instructor before Christ
5. Put right by faith
6. They turned to another gospel.
7. To pass it on
8. Last forever
9. Help each other carry.

C. FEATURES: Write the names of the basic Letters of Paul

1. _____ 2. _____ 3. _____ 4. _____

Identify each of the following items as a distinguishing feature of a particular basic Letter by writing the initial on the blank.

5. ___ Restoration of a broken relationship
6. ___ Written to introduce himself and his preaching
7. ___ To defend his apostleship and affirm the liberty of the gospel
8. ___ Answers questions and solves problems
9. ___ Probably composed of parts of different letters
10. ___ Factions were splitting the church.
11. ___ "Put right with God through faith" is a major theme.
12. ___ The cross as nonsense to those being lost
13. ___ Adam and Christ
14. ___ Grafting Gentiles; return of the Jews
15. ___ Love: patient, kind, eternal

16. ____ Reluctant display of credentials
17. ____ Autobiography
18. ____ Food offered to idols
19. ____ Carry each other's burdens.
20. ____ Speaking in tongues
21. ____ Legal disputes
22. ____ Gentiles and Jews told to accept each other.
23. ____ The Law or the Spirit
24. ____ Effects of faith
25. ____ Treasure in clay pots

Check answers on next page. Then compute scores and enter them on Unit 1 Growth Record below.

Category	# Correct	% Score	Directions
A. Structure	____ = ____		See chart below.
B. Teachings	____ = ____		# Correct times 3 = ___ + 1 = %
C. Features	____ = ____		# Correct times 4 = %
Total Score (A+B+C)	____ = ____		# Correct times 4 = ___ ÷ 3 = %

#	1	2	3	4	5	6	7	8	9	10	11	12	13	14	15	16	17	#
%	6	12	18	24	29	35	41	47	53	59	65	71	77	82	88	94	100	%

UNIT 1 GROWTH RECORD

For each test record your % scores for each category as well as total test score. To determine growth, subtract pre-test score from unit test score.

Category	Pre-test	Sect. 1	Sect. 2	Sect. 3	Sect. 4	Unit	Growth
Structure	%	%	%	%	%	%	%
Teachings							
Features		xxxxx	xxxxx	xxxxx			
Total							

Remember to look up references for any unit test items you missed. Then proceed with Unit 2.

49

ANSWERS TO UNIT TEST 1

A. STRUCTURE (17)

1. Doctrine
2. Put Right with God Through Faith
3. Promise to Israel
4. (Exhortation): Ethics
5. Disorders (reported in Corinth)
6. Answers to Questions (from Corinth)
7. Worship (Concerning)
8. Resurrection (of the dead)
9. Plans
10. Paul's Message and Mission
11. Separation and Purity
12. Restoration of Confidence
13. Offering
14. The Harsh Letter
15. Paul's Defense: Apostleship and Gospel
16. Doctrine: Law or Faith
17. Ethics: Freedom and Spirit

B. TEACHINGS (33)

1. e (2 Cor. 2:14)   6 (Rom 13:8)   4 (1 Cor. 6:19)   5 (Rom. 4:10)
2. a (Rom. 5--8)   3 (Rom. 3:24)   1 (1 Cor. 11:14-   8 (2 Cor. 4:18)
3. a (1 Cor. 6:7)   1 (Rom. 5:12-21)   16)   7 (2 Cor. 1:4)
4. c (1 Cor. 11--14)   7 (Rom. 7:6)   3 (1 Cor. 7:2,9)   1 (Rom. 7:10;
5. c (Gal. 4:21-31)   4 (Rom. 4:16;   7 (1 Cor. 11:29)   8:2)
6. e (Rom. 2:17-24;   Gal. 4:28)   2 (1 Cor. 14:5)   6 (Gal. 1:6)
     4:1-8)   2 (Rom. 3:20)   5 (1 Cor. 15:20)   9 (Gal. 6:2)
7. c (Rom. 11:25)   5 (Rom. 12:21)   6 (2 Cor. 6:14)   4 (Gal. 3:24)
8. e (1 Cor. 15)   3 (Gal. 5:6,
9. a (Gal. 5:22)   13)
10. b (2 Cor. 7:7)   2 (Gal. 1:15)

C. FEATURES (25)

1-4   (in any order) Rom., 1 Cor.,   15. 1 C   (13:4-8)
      2 Cor., Gal. (Text p. 4)   16. 2 C   (ch. 11)
5. 2 C   (7:8-16)   17. G   (1:11--2:14)
6. R   (1:1-15; 15:22-23)   18. 1 C   (ch. 8)
7. G   (chs. 1--2)   19. G   (6:2)
8. 1 C   (chs. 1--15)   20. 1 C   (ch. 14)
9. 2 C   (page 11)   21. 1 C   (6:1-8)
10. 1 C   (1:10-11)   22. R   (15:7-9)
11. R   (1:17)   23. G   (3:1-5)
12. 1 C   (1:18)   24. R   (chs. 5--8)
13. R   (5:12-15)   25. 2 C   (4:7)
14. R   (11:17)

UNIT 2: THE PRISON LETTERS

OBJECTIVES

After the completion of Unit 2 you will be able to do the following:

1. <u>State the headings</u> of the major divisions in each of the four Letters.

2. <u>Identify at least five persons</u> by matching them with associated descriptions or actions.

3. <u>Select the correct conclusion</u> for at least 20 partial teachings from the prison Letters.

4. <u>Identify the prison Letters</u> by name.

5. <u>Identify at least 10 themes or special content items</u> as belonging to a particular Letter.

6. <u>Identify</u> the general conclusions of scholarship concerning <u>authorship, readers, and purpose</u> in writing each of the prison Letters.

You will next take a pre-test as you did in Unit 1. Remember you are not expected to do well at all. The test is designed to be a learning experience giving you a preview of what you need to learn, guiding your later study, and demonstrating how your study has benefited you with increased knowledge at the end of the unit.

Now begin the pre-test for Unit 2.

PRE-TEST FOR UNIT 2: PRISON LETTERS

A. STRUCTURE: Circle the ONE BEST answer for each statement.

1. The major divisions of Ephesians are:
   a. Thanksgiving; Warnings
   b. Thanksgiving; Faith and Works
   c. Doctrine; Exhortation
   d. Circumcision Versus Resurrection; Instructions
   e. The Love of God; False Teachers

2. One major subdivision under each of the above two divisions:
   a. Mystery of Call of Gentiles; Unit of the Body
   b. Rejoice; Troublemakers
   c. Superiority of Christ; Duties of Elders
   d. Christian Blessings; Criteria for Teachers
   e. Abraham's Faith; A Personal Appeal

3. The three major divisions of Philippians include ALL of the following EXCEPT:
   a. News and Exhortation
   b. Warning Against Troublemakers
   c. Thanks for the Gift
   d. Final Instructions

4. The major divisions of Colossians include ALL of the following EXCEPT:
   a. Basis for Letter
   b. Warning Against False Teaching
   c. Paul's Example
   d. Exhortation: Ethics
   e. Conclusion

5. The major divisions of Philemon include ALL of the following EXCEPT:
   a. Subject: Onesimus
   b. Message from Philemon
   c. New Relationship
   d. Request: Welcome him.
   e. Anticipated Visit

B. NARRATIVES:
   Persons. Write the number of EACH person's name on the blank before the ONE term with which he is most closely associated.

   ____ A church leader
   ____ A runaway slave
   ____ Brought Paul gift from Philippi
   ____ Founded a church
   ____ Paul planned to send to Philippi

   1. Epaphras
   2. Timothy
   3. Philemon
   4. Epaphroditus
   5. Onesimus

C. TEACHINGS: Write the number of EACH partial teaching on the blank before the ONE term which most nearly completes it or with which it is most closely associated. Do each group separately.

   ____ Uniting all people in Christ
   ____ Christ
   ____ Completion of salvation
   ____ God chose Christians to be his own
   ____ Unnecessary
   ____ Union of Jews and Gentiles
   ____ Helmet

   1. Before the world was made
   2. God's purpose
   3. Law abolished
   4. Salvation
   5. Life to Paul
   6. Asceticism
   7. Keep working.

   ____ Lord of all
   ____ Head of body
   ____ Created in God's likeness
   ____ From Spirit
   ____ Strength to face all conditions
   ____ Belong to the light
   ____ Possessed by Christians

   1. Power from Christ
   2. Christ makes all parts grow.
   3. New self
   4. Christians
   5. Life and freedom
   6. Unity of body
   7. Christ

____ Reality	1. Eliminate bad feelings.
____ Fill your minds.	2. Paul's method
____ Put on new self.	3. Christ
____ Reach for what is ahead.	4. Prayer
____ Persist.	5. Shadows of reality
____ Jewish rules	6. Those things that are good

D. FEATURES: Write Eph., Phil., Col., or Philem., to identify each of the following items as distinguishing ONE of the prison Letters.

1. ____ Jewish Gnosticism, a problem

2. ____ A private letter

3. ____ May be more than one letter

4. ____ Probably intended for Christians in general

5. ____ Asks clemency for a slave

6. ____ One body

7. ____ Christ in first place

8. ____ Rejoice!

9. ____ Gift for Paul

10. ____ The belt of truth

11. ____ Visible likeness of the invisible God

12. ____ Welcome him as me.

13. ____ No power in circumcision or the Law

14. ____ God's saving gift of grace

15. ____ A church which Paul had never visited

16. ____ "Fill your mind with these things ..."

17. ____ "Live like people who belong to the light."

18. ____ " ... learned to be satisfied."

19. ____ Reality is Christ.

20. ____ The whole armor of God

Check your answers, and compute your scores on the next page.

ANSWERS TO PRE-TEST FOR UNIT 2

A. STRUCTURE (5)

1. c
2. a
3. d
4. c
5. b

B. NARRATIVES (5)

3
5
4
1
2

C. TEACHINGS (20)

2	7	3
5	2	6
7	3	1
1	6	2
6	1	4
3	4	5
4	5	

D. FEATURES (15)

1. Col.   11. Col.
2. Philem.   12. Philem.
3. Phil.   13. Phil.
4. Eph.   14. Eph.
5. Philem.   15. Col.
6. Eph.   16. Phil.
7. Col.   17. Eph.
8. Phil.   18. Phil.
9. Phil.   19. Col.
10. Eph.   20. Eph.

PRE-TEST SCORES FOR UNIT 2

Category	# Correct	% Score	Directions
A. Structure	____ = ____		# Correct times 20 = %
B. Narratives	____ = ____		# Correct times 20 = %
C. Teachings	____ = ____		# Correct times 5 = %
D. Features	____ = ____		Check % on chart below.
Total (A+B+C+D)	____ = ____		# Correct times 2 = %

#	1	2	3	4	5	6	7	8	9	10	11	12	13	14	15	#
%	7	13	20	26	33	40	46	53	60	67	73	80	86	93	100	%

Enter your % scores for each category and for the pre-test on the Unit 2 Growth Record, page 91.

UNIT 2: THE PRISON LETTERS

In Letters to the Ephesians, Philippians, Colossians, and Philemon, the writer mentions that he is in prison. Therefore this course has removed Philemon from its canonical order so that it can be included in this unit.

ACTS Records:
Caesarea A.D. 56-60
Rome A.D. 58-63

Scholarship:
Ephesus A.D. 50-55

Acts tells of two imprisonments for Paul, one in Caesarea (ca. A.D. 56-60) and the other in Rome (ca. A.D. 58-63). One second-century scholar and many modern scholars think there was a third imprisonment in Ephesus, about A.D. 52-55. The four prison Letters all begin with the signature of Paul, and his authorship was not questioned before the 19th century. If all were written by Paul, they must all be dated between A.D. 52 and 63 during the last part of Paul's life.

By Paul

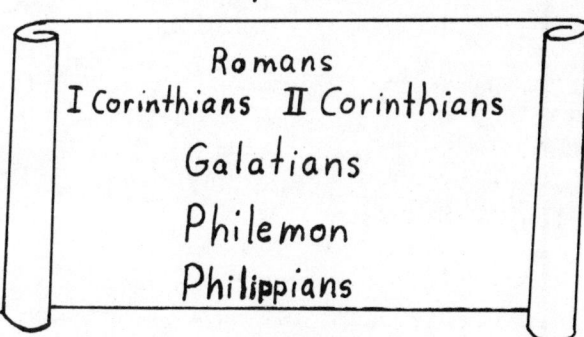

Romans
I Corinthians   II Corinthians
Galatians
Philemon
Philippians

That Philippians and Philemon were written by Paul is unquestioned by almost all authorities. Authorship of Ephesians and Colossians is debated by scholars. These letters may be pseudonymous (written in Paul's name as was sometimes done by a disciple delivering a teacher's message to a later day). If these two Letters were written by a later church leader, they may have been written between A.D. 80 and 100.

Debated: By a follower?

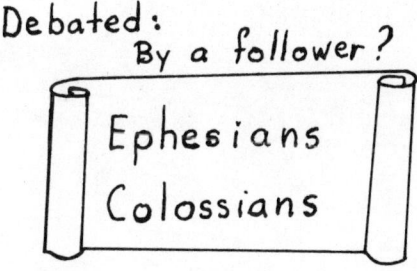

Ephesians
Colossians

Units 1 and 2 include all the Letters which are unquestionably ascribed to Paul and those which have a case for his authorship by reliable scholars.

Work through Unit 2 as you did Unit 1. (See instructions, page 10.)

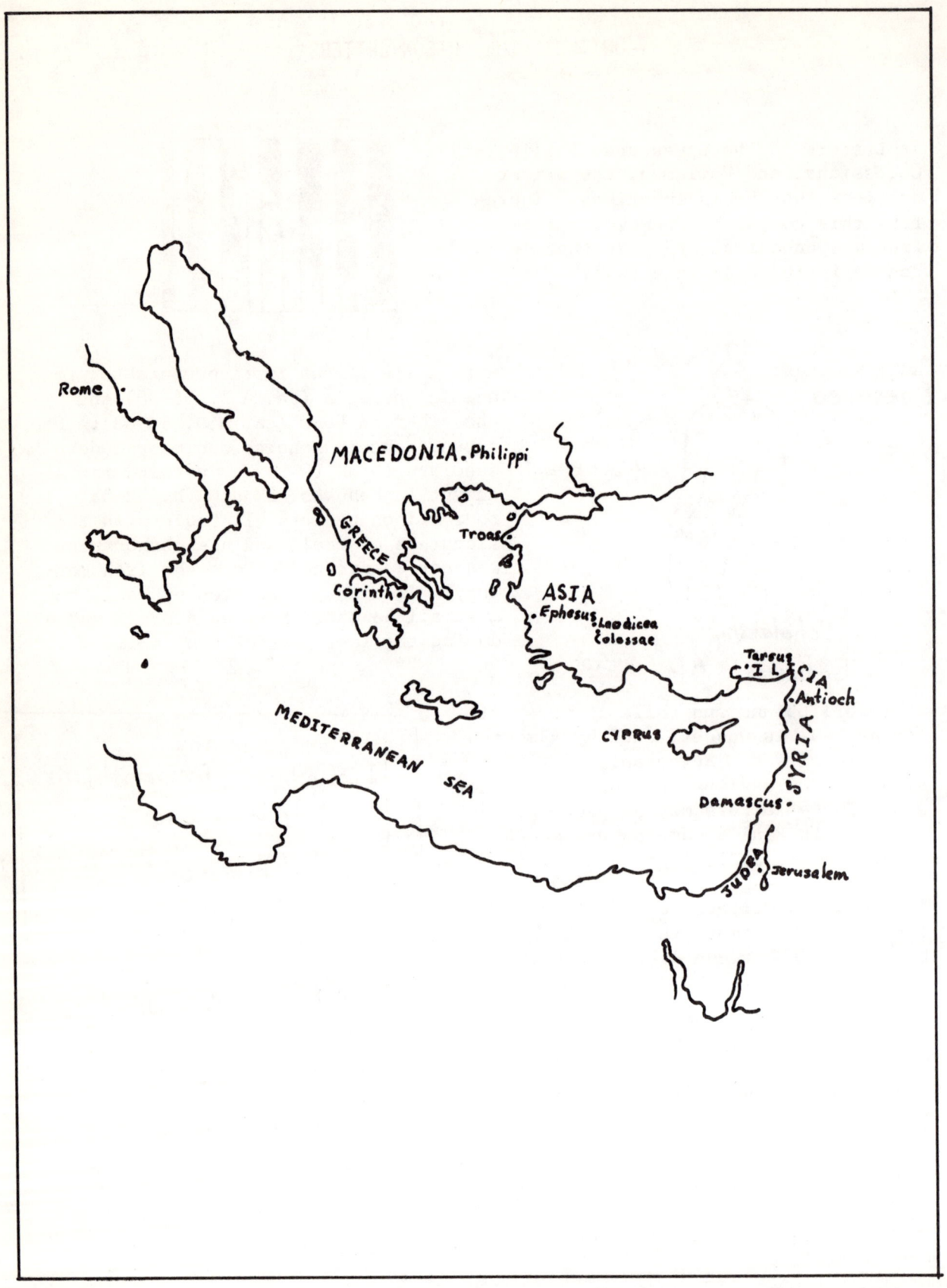

10   BACKGROUND OF EPHESIANS

AUTHOR: Paul, strongly debated today. Many think it is pseudonymous, that is, written in Paul's name by a follower delivering Paul's message to another day.
READERS: The mixed Jewish-Gentile church of Ephesus, but the original quite likely was intended for Christians in general
DATE AND PURPOSE: If by Paul, written from prison about the same time as Colossians and Philemon ca. A.D. 52-63 to reassure and instruct his friends. If by a later church leader, written in Asia Minor between A.D. 80 and 100 to celebrate unity of Jews and Gentiles in Christ.

20   BACKGROUND OF PHILIPPIANS

AUTHOR: Paul, undoubted
READERS: Church founded in Philippi, Macedonia
NATURE OF MATERIAL: Maybe a single letter; perhaps a compilation of three letters
DATE: One or more of Paul's imprisonments between A.D. 52 and 63. If three letters, perhaps from different places and times
PURPOSE: To thank the Philippian church for their gift, reassure them about their messenger's illness, to report on his own condition, and warn them against some troublemakers in Philippi--warmly personal letter(s).

30   BACKGROUND OF COLOSSIANS

AUTHOR: Paul, debated. Some think it is pseudonymous. (See line 1 above.)
READERS: Christians (mostly Gentiles) in Colossae, a church probably founded by Epaphras and never visited by Paul
CIRCUMSTANCES: Jewish legalism and Gnostic faith in semi-divine beings were taught in Colossae. Epaphras needed an authoritative word from Paul to combat these teachings.
DATE AND PURPOSE:
   If by Paul: dated with Philem. (same messenger, likely same town) during one of Paul's imprisonments, between A.D. 52 and 63. Written to combat Gnostic heresy
   If by a later church leader: date uncertain, but earlier than Ephesians. Brought ideas of Paul to combat Jewish Gnosticism.

40   BACKGROUND OF PHILEMON

AUTHOR: Paul, undoubted
READER: Philemon, a leader in a local church, likely at Colossae
   (Note: This is a personal letter not a church epistle.)

(Background continued on the next page.)

57

10 BACKGROUND OF EPHESIANS

1. Written by:
   a. Paul
   b. Peter
   c. Later church leader
   d. Anonymous
   e. a or c

2. Written
   a. From prison
   b. To reassure friends
   c. To celebrate unity
   d. a and (b or c)
   e. a, b, and c

Check answers from information on page 57, and proceed.

20 BACKGROUND OF PHILIPPIANS

1. Written by _____ to _____

2. This Letter differs from most by Paul in that:
   a. It gives a warning.
   b. It may be three letters.
   c. Paul talks about himself.
   d. It is a formal sermon.
   e. Paul closes with a benediction.

Check answers with information on page 57. If questions arise about wrong answers, see passages at right: Rom. 16:17   1 Cor. 9
2 Cor. 13:2   2 Cor. 11
Gal. 4:17   Gal. 2

30 BACKGROUND OF COLOSSIANS

1. Written by _____

2. Readers were:
   a. Christians at Colossae
   b. Mostly Gentiles
   c. Mostly Jews
   d. a and b
   e. a and c

3. Written to:
   a. Answer questions.
   b. Combat Jewish Gnosticism.
   c. Combat immorality.
   d. Combat dissension.
   e. Introduce a brother.

Check answers from information on page 57, and proceed.

40 BACKGROUND OF PHILEMON (continued)

CIRCUMSTANCES AND PURPOSE: Paul while in prison had met a runaway slave, Onesimus, whom he returned to his master, Philemon, with this Letter recommending clemency.

DATE AND PLACE OF WRITING: A prison epistle, written sometime during the period A.D. 52-63.

11   OPENING: 1:1-2

12   DOCTRINE: Faith and Principles: 1--3

12A Doxology: 1:3-14
     READ: Eph. 1

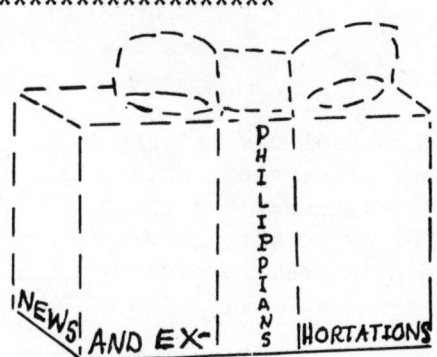

1. What does Paul say God did before the world was made?

2. What does the writer say is God's plan?

****

21   OPENING: PRAYER FOR READERS: 1:1-11

22   NEWS AND EXHORTATIONS: 1:12--2:8
     (Letter B?)

22A News. READ: Phil. 1:1-26

1. In what two ways did Paul's imprisonment help the gospel progress?

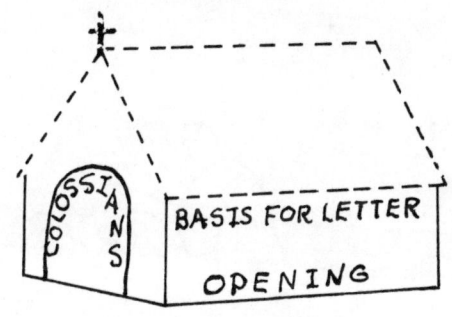

****

31   OPENING: 1:1-2

32   BASIS FOR LETTER
     READ: Col. 1:1--2:5

32A Thanksgiving: 1:3-8

Who first preached the gospel to the Colossians?

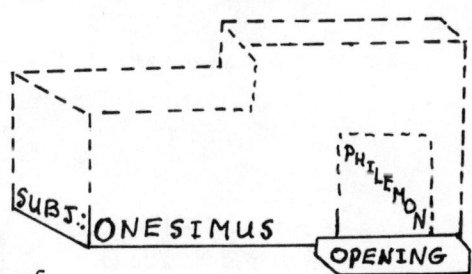

****

41   OPENING: Verses 1-17
     READ: The Letter to Philemon

42   MESSAGE: Verses 8-22

42A Subject: Onesimus: vss. 8-11

1. Making a request of Philemon instead of a demand, Paul wrote on behalf of Onesimus. Who was Onesimus and what had Paul become in relation to him?

12A

1. He chose Christians to be his own people.

2. To bring all creation together with Christ as head

****

22A

1. All knew Paul was in prison because of serving Christ, and his imprisonment had given his fellow workers more confidence in their preaching.

****

32A

    Epaphras (1:5, 7)

****

42A

1. Onesimus was a runaway slave. Paul had become his spiritual father.

12B   Prayer: 1:15-23

12C   Central Teaching: Mystery of the Call of the Gentiles
       READ: Eph. 2--3

1. How does Paul describe God's act of saving men through faith?

2. When Christ's death broke down the wall between Jew and Gentile, what did Christ abolish?

****

22A   News: 1:12-26

2. What was life to Paul?

22B   Exhortations: 1:27--2:18

1. What does Paul ask of the Philippians concerning the faith of the gospel?

****

32B   Prayer: 1:9-12

32C   Christology: 1:13-20

   The writer here gives a summary of his teaching about Christ. Verses 15-20 contain an early hymn.

1. The Jewish faith forbade any attempts to represent God's likeness. How does the teaching in this hymn modify the Jewish teaching?

2. What was Christ's role in creation?

****

42A   Subject: Onesimus: vss. 8-11

2. Instead of being useless, to whom was Onesimus now useful?

42B   Request: Return Him to Paul: vss. 12-14

1. Although Paul was sending Onesimus back to Philemon, what did he really want to do?

61

12C

1. It is by God's grace; it is God's gift.

2. The Law

****

22A

2. Christ

22B

1. To stand firm and to fight for it

****

32C

1. It says that Christ is the visible likeness of the invisible God.

2. By him God created everything.

****

42A

2. Both to Philemon and to Paul

42B

1. To keep Onesimus as his helper in prison

12C Mystery of the Call of the Gentiles

3. Why did Christ break down the wall and abolish the Law?

4. What did the writer say he was to do as servant of the gospel?

12D Prayer: 3:14-19

12E Doxology: 3:20-21

****

22B Exhortations: 1:27--2:18

2. Paul recorded a hymn about Christ. What two qualities does Paul say Jesus had which made his name greater than any other name?

3. Why did Paul say that the Philippians could keep working to complete their salvation?

****

32D Effect of the Gospel: 1:21-23

How were the Colossians changed from God's enemies to his friends?

32E Paul's Ministry: 1:24--2:5

What glorious secret does Paul say God has for all peoples (=Gentiles)?

****

42B Request: Return Him to Paul: vss. 12-14

2. What was the only way Paul would keep Onesimus?

42C New Relationship: vss. 15-16

What was the new relationship Onesimus would have with Philemon?

12C

3. To create a single new people; to unite the Jews and Gentiles in one body

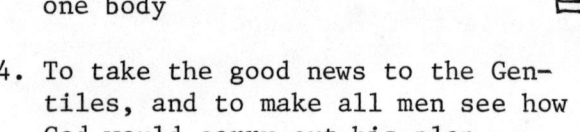 

4. To take the good news to the Gentiles, and to make all men see how God would carry out his plan

Turn to Section Chart 1 on page 75, and complete blanks 1-5. Check answers on page 78. Study the corrected chart, and continue on page 65.

****

22B

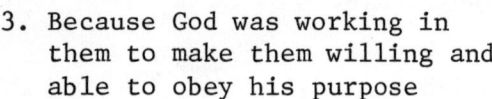

2. Humility and obedience

3. Because God was working in them to make them willing and able to obey his purpose

****

32D

By the physical death of his Son

32E

That Christ is in them (us) which means they (we) can share in the glory of God

****

42B

2. If this was Philemon's free will

42C

Brothers in Christ

Turn to Section Chart 4 on page 78, and complete blanks 1-6. Check your answers at the bottom of the page. Study the corrected chart, and continue work on page 65.

JUST FOR FUN!

Now that you've finished the first major section of Ephesians, perhaps you'd like to stop and think about it. (If you're in a hurry you can skip this part, or any "Just for Fun.") Reread Paul's prayers 1:15-19 and 3:14-21. Notice his emphases and main concerns. What do these prayers tell you about the person who prayed them?

Consider your own prayers. What do they tell you about yourself?

****

22C Travel Plans of Messengers: 2:19-30

1. Who was the messenger Paul was sending to get news of the Philippians?

2. Who was the Philippian messenger who almost died after he brought Paul the gift from the Philippians?

22D Final Exhortation: May the Lord give you much joy. 3:1
     (Is this concluded in 4:4-7?)

****

JUST FOR FUN!

Try this. Paul had many fellow workers, some of whom he took with him on his travels. In this way he trained leaders for the new churches. Look back through the openings and closings of the Basic and Prison Letters to see their names. (Also see Phil. 2:19 and 4:2.) Make a list and add any information you can find about each. Can you discover clues about Paul's attitudes toward fellow workers and his methods of developing leaders?

****

JUST FOR FUN!

This Letter names ten Christians in addition to Paul. Check your earlier list of Paul's fellow workers, and add all new names that you find in Philemon. Note which other Letter contains most of the names mentioned in Philemon.

JUST FOR FUN!

Ephesians is a letter that sings. Maybe you have heard George Beverly Shea sing "The Love of God." If you know the words, or can look them up, compare them with Ephesians 3:18. Other songs may have come to your mind as you read Ephesians, depending on your taste in music. Why not sing one of them to an appreciative audience--you. You might even make up your own song if Ephesians has given you something to sing about.

****

22C

1. Timothy

2. Epaphroditus

Turn to Section Chart 2 on page 76, and complete blanks 1-4. Check answers on page 78. Study the corrected chart, and continue work on page 67.

****

JUST FOR FUN!

Paul uses many metaphors or verbal images of abstractions. Remember the armor of God in Ephesians? Colossians has many verbal pictures of Christ. See how many you can find and draw rough sketches of them. For starters try 2:3 and 2:15b.

****

JUST FOR FUN!

Most of the time Timothy or another of Paul's assistants did the manual writing at Paul's direction. Philemon is one of the letters in which we have a record of Paul's writing words in his own hand. (Note 1 Cor. 16:21 and Gal. 6:11.)

Read what he writes in his own hand in Colossians and Philemon. Why do you think he wrote a few words this way?

13   EXHORTATION: LIFE AND PRACTICE: 3--4
       READ: Eph. 4
13A   The Unity of the Body: 4:1-16

1. What did Paul urge the Ephesians to preserve?

2. How is Christ related to the body?
   (... and so makes it grow in love.)

****

JUST FOR FUN!

Philippians is rich in quotations which Christians have found helpful for centuries. When you look back over the first two chapters, do you find a verse or a sentence or a passage which you would like to remember? Memorize it, and it's yours! You <u>could</u> do this later for the last two chapters too.

****

33   WARNING AGAINST FALSE TEACHING
       READ: Col. 2:6-23

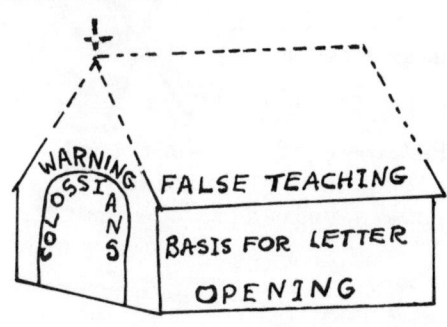

33A   Exhortation
       Live in Union with Christ: 2:6-7

33B   "Ruling Spirits" Versus Christ: 2:8-15

1. What did Paul warn the Colossians not to accept?

2. From what power did Christ free himself on the cross?

33C   Implication of Christ's Superiority: 2:16-23

Paul warned against circumcision, severe treatment of the body, and other legalistic religious practices. Why did he call the Jewish Law a shadow of reality and the practices both ineffective and unnecessary?

****

42D   Request Continued: Welcome Him! vss. 17-20

1. What did Paul ask Philemon to do concerning Onesimus and anything Onesimus owed Philemon?

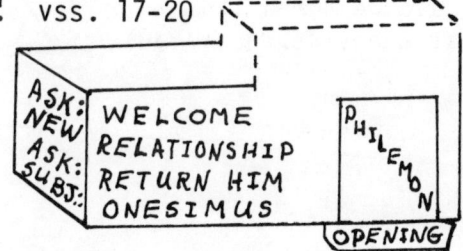

13A

1. The unity of the body

2. He is the head of it.

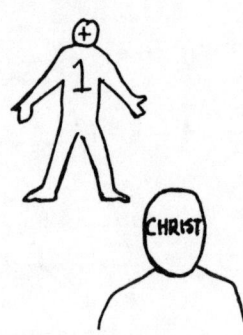

****

JUST FOR FUN!

In 2:1-17 Paul gives his conception of the way Christians should live based upon Christ's example. Go through a typical day in your life (yesterday or a day last week), and at each point go over Paul's list. How would your day have been different if you had always applied his teachings? (Note: "You" is plural throughout this passage. Read it for yourself as an individual <u>in a community</u>.)

****

33B

1. Human wisdom

2. The power of the spiritual rulers and authorities (powers valued by the Gnostics)

33C

Because the Colossians already had life and freedom in Christ: Reality is Christ.

Turn to Section Chart 3 on page 77, and complete blanks 1-8. Check answers on page 78. Study the corrected chart, and continue on page 69.

****

42D

1. To welcome back Onesimus as he would have welcomed Paul and to charge any debts to Paul

13B The New Life in Christ: 4:17-32

As members of the body of Christ, Paul said the Ephesians must put on a new self. What was this self like?

13C Living in the Light. READ: Eph. 5:1-20

Since the Gentiles had been brought out of darkness, what were they told to do?

****

23 WARNING AGAINST TROUBLEMAKERS (Letter C ?)
    READ: Phil. 3:2--4:9

23A Circumcision Versus Resurrection: 3:2-11

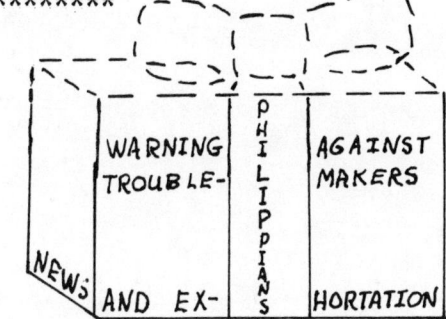

Paul warns against those who wanted to circumcise. What does he say is the source of power instead of the Law?

23B Paul's Struggle Toward the Goal: 3:12-16

What is the one thing Paul says he was doing in striving to reach his goal?

****

34 EXHORTATION: ETHICS. READ: Col. 3:1--4:6

34A Life of Those Raised with Christ: 3:1-17

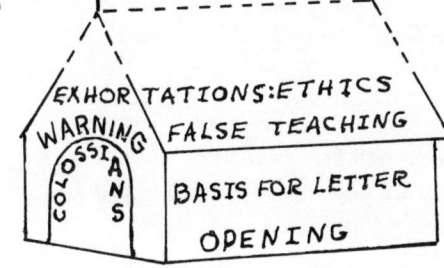

1. After telling the Colossians to keep their minds set on heaven, why does Paul tell them to get rid of hateful feelings?

2. What is the result of God's constant renewal of man in his own image?

34B Household Relationships: 3:18--4:1

This passage is like Ephesians 5:21--6:9   (See 13D, p. 71.)

34C In General: Prayer, Conduct, Speech: 4:2-6

After advising persistence in prayer, what did Paul advise in working with unbelievers?

****

42D Request Continued: vss. 18-21

2. Philemon, a fellow Christian, owed Paul his life. How did Paul expect Philemon to respond to his requests?

13B

In God's likeness, revealed
in upright and holy life

13C

To live like people who
belonged to the light

****

23A

Christ's resurrection

23B

He was trying to forget what was
behind and to reach what was ahead.

****

34A

1. Because they have to put off the
   old self and put on the new
   (Eph. 4:22-24 speaks of this.)

2. There is no more Jew or
   Gentile, slave or free.
   Christ is all and in all.

34C

To be wise in action

****

42D

2. Paul was sure that Philemon would
   do even more than Paul had asked.

13D Household Relationships: READ: Eph. 5:21--6:9

1. Paul describes the relationship between Christ and his church as analogous to that between man and wife. How were husbands and wives told to show their reverence for Christ?

2. What were parents told to avoid?

3. What were slaves and masters told to remember?

****

23C A Personal Appeal: Stand Firm: 3:17--4:3

   After reminding the Philippians that they are citizens of heaven, in what does he ask them to stand firm?

23D Rejoice! 4:4-7
     (Does this conclude in 3:1?)

23E Final Exhortation: Fill your minds . . . 4:8-9

****

35 CONCLUSION. READ: Col. 4:7-18

35A News: 4:7-9

   Who would tell the Colossians the news about Paul?

35B Greetings and Instructions: 4:10-17

   What church would exchange readings of Paul's Letters with the Colossian church?

****

42E Anticipated Visit: vss. 21-22

   What did Paul ask Philemon to do in the hope that God would answer their prayers?

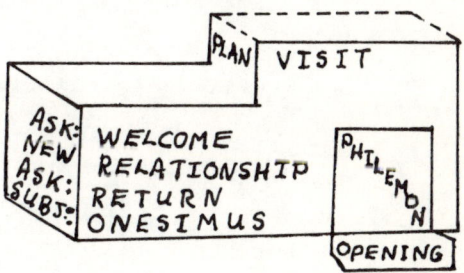

71

13D

1. To submit to each other

2. Making their children angry

3. That they belong to the same Master in heaven who treats all alike

****

23C

In their life in the Lord

Another Just for Fun!

You are about to read the "thank you" part of Philippians. It still feels good to read such a letter. Why not stop thinking about the Bible long enough to write a letter to someone who has done something nice for you? "Doing the truth" in that way might spread some of the joy you're reading about. Try it, just for fun!

****

35A

Tychicus and Onesimus

35B

Laodicea

****

42E

Get a room ready for him.

13E The Whole Armor of God.   READ: 6:10-20

1. After telling the Ephesians to use God's power, what qualities did Paul give as the six parts of the armor of God?

2. Where did the writer say he was?

14 CLOSING: 6:21-23

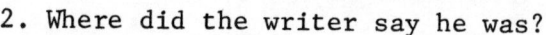

****

24 THANKS FOR THE GIFT: 4:10-20
    (Letter A?) READ: Phil. 4:10-23

1. In thanking the Philippians for the gift Epaphroditus had brought to Paul in prison, what does Paul say he has learned in life?

2. What does Paul say Christ's power enables him to do?

3. What does Paul say God will do for the Philippians?

25 CLOSING: 4:21-23

****

36 CLOSING: 4:18

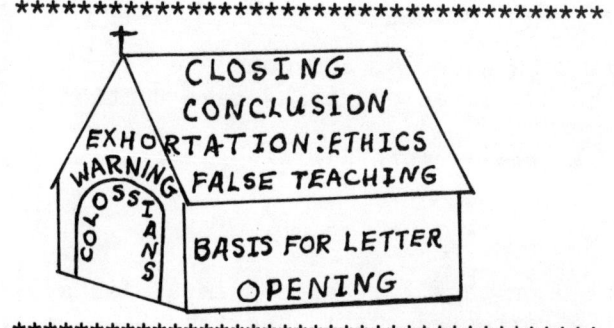

****

43 CLOSING: Verses 23-25

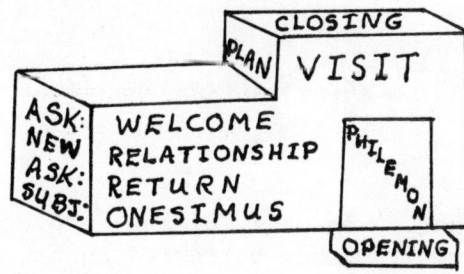

13E

1. Truth, righteousness, readiness to announce the gospel, faith, salvation, and the Word of God

2. In prison

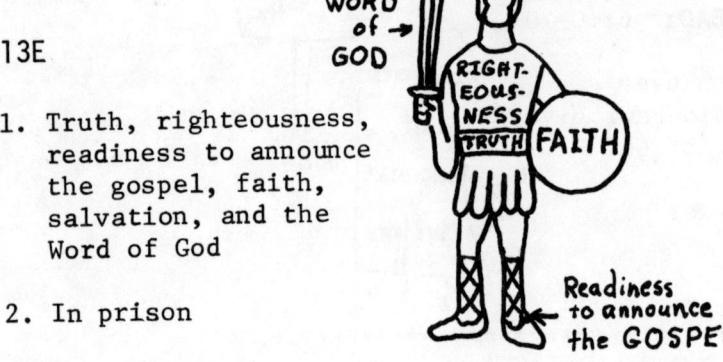

Turn to Section Chart 1 on page 75, and complete blanks 6-15. Check answers on page 78. Study the corrected chart, and take Section Test 1 on page 79.

****

24

1. To be satisfied with what he has

2. To face all conditions

3. He will supply all their needs.

Turn to Section Chart 2 on page 76, and complete blanks 5-10. Check answers on page 78. Study the corrected chart, and take Section Test 2 on page 81.

****

Turn to Section Chart 3 on page 77, and complete blanks 9-10. Check answers on page 78. Study the corrected chart, and take Section Test 3 on page 83.

****

Turn to Section Chart 4 on page 78, and complete blanks 7-9. Check answers (printed upside down). Study corrected chart, and take Section Test 4 on page 84.

SECTION CHART 1: EPHESIANS

_____
OPENING
DOCTRINE (1--3)

Chs.

CHOOSING AND SAVING PURPOSE

1

God chose Christians   [CHRIST]   God's plan: to bring
as his (1) _____   (2) _____
                                                   together with Christ
                                                   as head

       MYSTERY OF THE   [JEWS | ONE CHURCH | GENTILES]   CALL OF THE GENTILES

2

         Saved by grace   through faith

               All one   in Christ

             Christ's death   abolished the (3) _____
And united (4) _____   and Gentiles.

              Servant of   the secret plan

3   Paul to preach   the gospel to the Gentiles

    And to show all men how   (5) _____ would be
                                                        carried out

_____
EXHORTATION (4--6)

Christians to
  preserve: [CHRIST]   Christ is (7) _____
  (6) _____   of his body, the church,
4   making all grow in love.

          Put on a new self   in God's likeness,
                            [ONE BODY NEW LIFE]   upright and holy.

         Gentiles brought   from darkness
    Now, live like people   who belong to (8) _____
5

             Household   Relationships:
        Wives/husbands   Analogous to Christ/church

            Whole Armor   of God
6
    (9) _____;   Gospel; (10) _____
      Righteousness;   Salvation; Word

_____
CLOSING

Check answers on page 78, and study corrected chart.

SECTION CHART 2: PHILIPPIANS

OPENING: Prayer

1-2 — LETTER B ?

NEWS

Bolder (1) _____ about Christ

To (2) _____ is Christ

EXHORTATIONS

Stand firm!

Hymn: Christ's humility and obedience

Work out your own (3) _____

(4) _____ PLANS

Timothy: To Philippi

Epaphroditus: Ill messenger from Philippi

The Lord give you joy!

3-4:9 — LETTER C ?

(5) _____ AGAINST TROUBLEMAKERS

(6) _____ Versus Resurrection

Paul's struggle toward the (7) _____

Stand firm!

Rejoice!

Fill your (8) _____ with these things.

4:10-4:23 — LETTER A ?

THANKS FOR (9) _____

Can do all things

God (10) _____ your every need.

_____

Check answers on page 78, and study corrected chart.

SECTION CHART 3: COLOSSIANS

OPENING: 1:1-2

BASIS FOR LETTER 1:3--2:5

CHRIST IN FIRST PLACE

Christ is visible likeness of (1) _____

EFFECT OF CHRIST'S DEATH

God's enemies are made his (2) _____

Cross brings universe back to God.

MINISTRY OF PAUL

Telling God's Secret: (3) _____ is in all.

AGAINST FALSE TEACHING: 2:6-2:23

Human (4) _____

Circumcision _____

Jewish rules _____

Non-Christian teachings are (6) _____

R
e
a
l
CHRiST
t
y
i
s

Worship of angels

(5) _____ treatment of body

of reality, ineffective and (7) _____

Christians have life and (8) _____ in Christ.

EXHORTATION: ETHICS: 3:1-17

LIFE WHEN RAISED WITH CHRIST

Put off old self.
Put on new self.

God's (9) _____ of men:

No Jew No Gentile

Christ is All.

Household Relationships

IN GENERAL

Persistence in Prayer

(10) _____ in working with unbelievers

| News | CONCLUSION | Greetings |

CLOSING: 4:18

Check answers on page 78, and study corrected chart.

77

SECTION CHART 4: PHILEMON

OPENING: Verses 1-7
BODY: Verses 8-22

To (1) _____

SUBJECT:

(2) _____

REQUEST:

(5) _____
Onesimus to Paul

REQUEST CONTINUED:

(7) _____ him

(8) _____ to Paul any debts

Paul: His

(3) _____

Onesimus now

(4) _____ both

to Paul and Philemon

NEW RELATIONSHIP:

(6) _____

VISIT
Prepare (9) _____

CLOSING: Verses 23-25

ANSWERS TO SECTION CHARTS

Ephesians	Philippians	Colossians	Philemon
1. People (sons)	1. Preaching	1. God	1. Philemon
2. All creation	2. Live	2. Friends	2. Onesimus
3. Law	3. Salvation	3. Christ	3. Spiritual father
4. Jews	4. Travel	4. Wisdom	4. Useful
5. God's plan	5. Warning	5. Severe	5. Return
6. Unity	6. Circumcision	6. Shadows	6. Brothers in Christ
7. Head	7. Goal	7. Unnecessary	7. Welcome
8. Light	8. Minds	8. Freedom	8. Charge
9. Faith	9. Gift	9. Renewal	9. Room
10. Truth	10. Will supply	10. Wisdom	

SECTION TEST 1: EPHESIANS

A. STRUCTURE: Fill in the blanks in this outline of Ephesians.

   Opening

I. (1) _____
   A. Doxology
   B. Prayer
   C. Central Teaching: (2) _____
   D. Prayer
   E. Doxology

II. (3) _____
   A. (4) _____
   B. The New Life in Christ
   C. Living in the Light
   D. Household Relationships
   E. Concluding Image: (5) _____

C. TEACHINGS: Circle the ONE BEST answer for each statement.

1. In Ephesians Paul says that before the world was made God:
   a. Alone existed
   b. Planned to eliminate evil
   c. Set aside Israel to be his holy nation
   d. Chose Christians to be his people
   e. Created man

2. Paul says God's saving purpose is:
   a. To unite all people in Christ
   b. To enable man to earn his reward
   c. To redeem Gentiles in place of the Jews
   d. To destroy the present world
   e. a and b.

3. Christ abolished the Law
   a. To punish the Jews
   b. To reward the Gentiles
   c. To unite Jews and Gentiles
   d. Because it was bad
   e. All of the above

4. The whole armor of God includes ALL of the following EXCEPT:
   a. Salvation as a helmet
   b. Wisdom as a breastplate
   c. Truth as a belt
   d. Readiness to announce the good news of peace as shoes
   e. The Word of God as a sword

Write the number of EACH partial teaching in the blank before the term with which it is most closely associated.

    _____ Life in Christ
    _____ Reverence for Christ
    _____ Body grows in love.
    _____ Same Master
    _____ Living in the light
    _____ Unity given by Spirit

1. Ephesians to preserve
2. Christ is the head.
3. New self in God's likeness
4. Those who turned from dark deeds
5. Submission of husband and wife to each other
6. Slave and owner

FEATURES:

Background: Circle the ONE BEST answer to each statement.

1. This Letter written to the church at Ephesus was:
   a. By Paul
   b. Pseudonymous
   c. Anonymous
   d. a or b
   e. a or b or c

2. Ephesians was written to:
   a. Reassure friends and instruct them.
   b. Appeal for help as Paul was in prison
   c. Celebrate unity in Christ.
   d. Explain difference between freedom from Law and license to sin.
   e. a or c

Special Content and Themes: Circle the numbers of eight features of Ephesians which distinguish it from the Basic Letters.

1. To a church Paul had not visited
2. May be more than one letter
3. Written from prison
4. One body in Christ
5. To answer questions
6. Saved by grace as God's gift
7. Adam and Christ
8. Put on a new self.
9. Don't make your children angry.
10. Conquer evil with good.
11. Divisions in the church
12. Live as belonging to the light.
13. Paul's autobiography
14. Nothing can separate us from God's love.
15. Husband/wife analagous to Christ/church
16. The shield of faith

Check answers on page 86, and compute scores on page 87.

SECTION TEST 2: PHILIPPIANS

A. STRUCTURE: Fill in the blanks in this outline of Philippians.

Opening

I. (1) _____
   A. News
   B. Exhortation
   C. Travel Plans of Messengers
   D. Final Exhortation: Rejoice!

II. (2) _____
   A. (3) _____ Versus Resurrection
   B. (4) _____ Toward Goal
   C. Personal Appeal: Stand Firm!
   D. Rejoice!
   E. Final Exhortation: Think about these things ...

III. (5) _____

Closing

B. NARRATIVES:

Persons: Write the number of EACH person or group on the blank before the ONE phrase with which it is most closely associated.

____ Paul's messenger to Philippi   1. Philippians
____ Helped Paul   2. Paul's fellow workers
____ Thanked Philippians for gift   3. Timothy
____ Almost died   4. Epaphroditus
____ Preached with more confidence   5. Paul

C. TEACHINGS: Circle the ONE BEST answer.

1. To Paul life is:
   a. Victories
   b. Christ
   c. Love
   d. Working for God
   e. Being oneself

2. Paul says the name of Jesus has been made greater than any other:
   a. In a hymn
   b. Because of his humility and obedience
   c. So no other man should be named Jesus
   d. So believers receive power by calling themselves Christians
   e. a and b

81

3. The Philippians were told to keep on working:
   a. To preach the gospel
   b. To help Paul and his fellow workers
   c. To complete their salvation
   d. a and b
   e. a, b, and c

4. Paul says power comes not through circumcision and the Law but through:
   a. Christ's resurrection
   b. Prayer
   c. The Scriptures
   d. Good works in Christ's name
   e. All of the above

5. Paul says his method of trying to win life with God is:
   a. To rely on Christ
   b. To forget the past
   c. To reach for the future
   d. To head straight for his goal
   e. b, c, and d

D. FEATURES: Circle the numbers of five features of Philippians which distinguish it from Ephesians.

1. All agree it is written by Paul.

2. Some say it is pseudonymous.

3. Stresses the unity of the body

4. May be parts of three letters

5. "Fill your minds with those things ..."

6. "God's plan ... to bring all creation together...."

7. "Learned to be satisfied"

8. "Put on all the armor that God gives you."

9. "Strength to face all conditions"

10. "Live like people who belong to the light."

Check your answers on page 86, and compute your scores on page 87.

SECTION TEST 3: COLOSSIANS

A. STRUCTURE: Fill in the blanks in this outline of Colossians.
    Opening
  I. (1) _____ for the _____

 II. Warning Against (2) _____

III. Exhortation: (3) _____

    A. Life (4) _____

    B. (5) _____ Relationships

    C. In General: Prayer, Conduct, Speech

 IV. Conclusion: News and Greetings

    Closing

C. TEACHINGS: Circle the ONE BEST answer to each statement.

1. Paul speaks of Christ in ALL of the following ways EXCEPT:
    a. Christ is the visible image of the invisible God.
    b. In the words of an early hymn
    c. Christ is the lamb of God.
    d. Christ's death made God's enemies his friends.
    e. Christ is all.

2. God's secret: Each person can share in God's glory by faith because:
    a. Christ has taught men rules to live by.
    b. Christ lives in each person.
    c. Faith is stronger than wisdom.
    d. Men are now partly divine.
    e. Christians are free from the Law.

3. Paul warned the Colossians against ALL of the following EXCEPT:
    a. Required observance of Jewish holy days
    b. False humility
    c. Worship of angels
    d. Those who cause divisions
    e. Human wisdom

4. The application of love to household relationships included ALL of the
   following EXCEPT:
    a. Husband-wife
    b. Parent-child
    c. Brother-sister
    d. Master-slave
    e. All of the above are included.

Write the number of EACH partial teaching in the blank before the ONE
term with which it is most closely associated.

____ Christ	1.	Christian
____ Prayer	2.	Jewish Law and customs
____ In working with unbelievers	3.	Reality
____ Life and freedom	4.	Severe treatment of body
____ Ineffective and unnecessary	5.	Wisdom
____ Shadows of reality	6.	Persistence

D. FEATURES: Circle the numbers of five features of Colossians which
    distinguish it from Ephesians and Philippians.

1. To a church founded by Paul
2. To a church likely founded by
   Epaphras
3. To combat Jewish and Gnostic
   ideas
4. Undoubtedly written by Paul
5. Anonymous

6. Workshop of angels, ruling spirits
7. Unity of the body
8. Christ in first place
9. Thanks for the gift
10. Reality is Christ.

Check your answers on page 86, and compute your scores on page 87.

SECTION TEST 4: PHILEMON

A. STRUCTURE: Fill in the blanks in this outline of Philemon.

Opening

Body of Letter

    A. Subject: (1) _____

    B. (2) _____

    C. (3) _____

    D. (4) _____

    E. Anticipated (5) _____

Closing

B. NARRATIVES:

Persons: Write O, Ph, or P in each blank to identify each phrase as most closely associated with Onesimus, Philemon, or Paul.

____ Letter sent to him
____ Met Onesimus in prison
____ A runaway slave
____ Requests welcome for O.
____ Wants Onesimus' help

____ Owes his life to Paul
____ Now useful
____ May owe money
____ Would be accepting a brother
____ Will pay any debts

D. FEATURES: Circle the ONE BEST answer to each statement.

1. Letter was written to:
   a. A church in Asia Minor
   b. A group of believers
   c. Christians in general
   d. An individual Christian
   e. A pagan man

2. Author of Letter is:
   a. Paul
   b. A disciple of Paul's
   c. Anonymous
   d. Pseudonymous
   e. Debated

3. Letter delivered by:
   a. Subject of Letter
   b. Onesimus
   c. Runaway slave
   d. Philemon's new brother
   e. All of above

4. The purpose of the Letter is:
   a. News of slave's whereabouts
   b. Request for return of slave
   c. Request to welcome him
   d. Offer to help
   e. b and c

5. Philemon was:
   a. A slave
   b. A church leader
   c. A brother in prison
   d. A church
   e. A city

Check your answers on page 86, and compute your scores below.

Category	# Correct	% Score	Directions
A. Structure	____ = ____		# Correct times 20 = %
B. Narratives	____ = ____		# Correct times 10 = %
D. Features	____ = ____		# Correct times 20 = %
Total (A+B+D)	____ = ____		# Correct times 5 = %

Enter your % scores for each category and for the section on the Unit 2 Growth Record, page 91. Review any material missed and then start Unit Test 2 on page 88.

ANSWERS TO SECTION TESTS

Test 1: Ephesians

A. STRUCTURE (5)

1. Doctrine: Faith and Principles
2. Mystery of the Call of the Gentiles
3. Exhortation: Life and Practice
4. Unity of the Body
5. Armor of God

C. TEACHINGS (5)

1. d   3
2. a   5
3. c   2
4. b   6
        4
        1

D. FEATURES (10)

Background (2)
1. d
2. e

Content/Theme (8)
3   9
4   12
6   15
8   16

Test 2: Philippians

A. STRUCTURE (5)

1. News and Exhortation
2. Warning Against Troublemakers
3. Circumcision
4. Paul's Struggle
5. Thanks for the Gift

B. NARRATIVES (5)

3
1
5
4
2

C. TEACHINGS (5)

1.b, 2.e, 3.c, 4.a, 5.e

D. FEATURES (5)

1   4   5   7   9

Test 3: Colossians

A. STRUCTURE (5)

1. Basis for the Letter
2. False Teaching
3. Ethics
4. In Christ
5. Household

C. TEACHINGS (10)

1. c   3
2. b   6
3. d   5
4. c   1
        4
        2

D. FEATURES (5)

2
3
6
8
10

Test 4: Philemon

A. STRUCTURE (5)

1. Onesimus
2. Request: Return him to Paul.
3. New Relationship
4. Request continued: Welcome him!
5. Visit

B. NARRATIVES (10)

Ph   Ph
P   O
O   O
P   Ph
P   P

D. FEATURES (5)

1. d
2. a
3. e
4. e
5. b

SECTION TEST SCORES

Test 1: Ephesians

Category	# Correct	% Score	Directions
A. Structure	___ = ___		# Correct times 20 = %
C. Teachings	___ = ___		# Correct times 10 = %
D. Features	___ = ___		# Correct times 10 = %
Total (A+C+D)	___ = ___		# Correct times 4 = %

Enter your % scores for each category and for the section on the Unit 2 Growth Record, page 91. Review any material missed, and then start Section 2, Philippians, on page 57.

Test 2: Philippians

Category	# Correct	% Score	Directions
A. Structure	___ = ___		# Correct times 20 = %
B. Narratives	___ = ___		# Correct times 20 = %
C. Teachings	___ = ___		# Correct times 20 = %
D. Features	___ = ___		# Correct times 20 = %
Total (A+B+C+D)	___ = ___		# Correct times 5 = %

Enter your % scores for each category and for the section on the Unit 2 Growth Record, page 91. Review any material missed, and then start Section 3, Colossians, on page 57.

Test 3: Colossians

Category	# Correct	% Score	Directions
A. Structure	___ = ___		# Correct times 20 = %
C. Teachings	___ = ___		# Correct times 10 = %
D. Features	___ = ___		# Correct times 20 = %
Total (A+C+D)	___ = ___		# Correct times 5 = %

Enter your % scores for each category and for the section on the Unit 2 Growth Record, page 91. Review any material missed, and then start Section 4, Philemon, on page 57. (Score chart for Test 4: Philemon, is on page 85.)

UNIT TEST 2

A. STRUCTURE: Fill in the blanks with the major headings of each Prison Letter.

Ephesians

I. (1) _____ : _____ and _____

II. (2) _____ : _____ and _____

Philippians

I. (3) _____ and _____

II. (4) _____ against _____

III. (5) _____ for the _____

Colossians

I. (6) _____ for _____ : _____ over _____

II. (7) _____ against _____

III. (8) _____ : _____

IV. Conclusion: News and Instructions

Philemon

A. Subject: (9) _____

B. Request: Return him to me.

C. New (10) _____

D. Request Continued: Welcome him!

E. Anticipated Visit

B. NARRATIVES:

Person: Write the number of EACH person on the blank in front of the ONE term most closely associated with that person.

____ Brought a gift from Philippi   1. Timothy
____ Paul's messenger to Philippi   2. Philemon
____ A runaway slave   3. Epaphroditus
____ Christian owner of slave   4. Epaphras
____ Probably founded church at Colossae   5. Onesimus

C. TEACHINGS: Circle the ONE BEST answer for each statement.

1. In Ephesians Paul says that before the world was made:
   a. Christ was born.
   b. God had established the Law.
   c. The church existed.
   d. Christians had been chosen to be God's people.
   e. All of the above

2. In Ephesians the mystery of God's call and his secret plan are Paul's references to:
   a. The bringing together of all creation in Christ
   b. Paul's conversion
   c. The restoration of Israel
   d. Isaiah's prophecies
   e. The crucifixion

3. Paul said the Colossians had to get rid of earthly desires and bad feelings because:
   a. They had put on a new self.
   b. They had put off the old self
   c. It was the way they could earn their salvation.
   d. a and b
   e. a, b, and c

4. When Paul told the Ephesians to put on a new self, he said it was:
   a. Created in God's likeness
   b. The resurrected body
   c. Revealed by God to all men
   d. Revealed in upright and holy living
   e. a and d

5. In Colossians Paul told God's glorious secret for all people:
   a. Christ rose from the dead.
   b. Christ rules all things.
   c. Christ is in you.
   d. God loves Gentiles as well as Jews.
   e. a and b

6. The armor of God includes ALL of the following EXCEPT:
   a. Faith
   b. Prayer
   c. Salvation
   d. Truth
   e. Word of God

7. To Paul life is:
   a. Loving one's neighbor
   b. Preaching the gospel
   c. Truth
   d. Christ
   e. Faith and love

8. Paul says that some rules (Ex. circumcision, asceticism)
   a. Are unnecessary
   b. Sometimes help
   c. Have a Christian meaning
   d. Interfere with God's power
   e. b and c

89

In each of the following groups write the number of each partial teaching on the blank before the phrase with which it is most closely associated. Use EACH name ONCE unless marked TWICE.

____ To complete salvation
____ To unite Jew and Gentile
____ As those who belong to light
____ Given by the Spirit
____ Through Christ's resurrection
____ Head of the body

1. Abolished the Law
2. Unity of Christians
3. Christ
4. Christians should live.
5. Keep working.
6. Power comes.

____ Persistence necessary
____ Lord of all
____ Jewish rules
____ Reach toward what is ahead.
____ Reality
____ Possessed by Christians

1. Forget the past.
2. Christ (Use twice.)
3. Prayer
4. Life and freedom
5. Shadows of reality

D. FEATURES: Write the names of the Prison Letters:

1. _____   3. _____

2. _____   4. _____

Identify each of the following items as a distinguishing feature of a particular Prison Letter by writing the initial of that Letter on the blank.

5. ____ May be three letters

6. ____ To combat Jewish and Gnostic ideas

7. ____ Probably intended for Christians in general

8. ____ A private letter

9. ____ One body in Christ

10. ____ A thank-you letter

11. ____ Christ in first place

12. ____ Rejoice!

13. ____ Saved through faith

14. ____ Reality is Christ.

15. ____ Paul as spiritual father

Check your answers on page 92, and compute your scores on page 91.

UNIT TEST 2 SCORES

Write the number correct (#) in each category. Multiply by the figure indicated at the right, and write your percent score for each category in the % blank. Add the # column and calculate your total % score as indicated. Then record your % scores on the Unit 2 Growth Record below.

Category	# Correct	% Score	Directions
A. Structure	____	= ____	# Correct times 10 = %
B. Narratives	____	= ____	# Correct times 20 = %
C. Teachings	____	= ____	# Correct times 5 = %
D. Features	____	= ____	See chart below.
Total (A+B+C+D)	____	= ____	# Correct times 2 = %

#	1	2	3	4	5	6	7	8	9	10	11	12	13	14	15	#
%	7	13	20	26	33	40	46	53	60	67	73	80	86	93	100	%

UNIT 2 GROWTH RECORD

For each test record your % scores for each category as well as total test score. To determine growth, substract pre-test score from unit test score.

Category	Pre-test	Eph.	Phil.	Col.	Philem.	Unit	Growth
A. Structure	%	%	%	%	%	%	%
B. Narratives		xxxx		xxxx			
C. Teachings					xxxx		
D. Features							
E. Total							

ANSWERS TO UNIT TEST 2

A. STRUCTURE (10)

(See headings and charts for references.)
1. Doctrine: Faith and Principles
2. Exhortation: Life and Practice
3. News and Exhortation
4. Warning Against Troublemakers
5. Thanks for the Gift
6. Basis for Letter
7. Warning Against False Teaching
8. Exhortation: Ethics
9. Onesimus
10. Relationship

B. NARRATIVES (5)

3 (Phil. 4:18)
1 (Phil. 2:19)
5 (Philem. 15-16)
2 (Philem. 16)
4 (Col. 1:7)

C. TEACHINGS (20)

1. d (Eph. 1:4)
2. a (Eph. 1:10)
3. d (Col. 3:8-9)
4. e (Eph. 4:24)
5. c (Col. 1:27)
6. b (Eph. 6:14-17)
7. d (Phil. 1:21)
8. a (Col. 2:17)

5 (Phil. 2:12)
1 (Eph. 2:15)
4 (Eph. 5:8)
2 (Eph. 4:3)
6 (Phil. 3:3-10)
3 (Eph. 4:15-16)

3 (Col. 4:2)
2 (Eph. 1:22)
5 (Col. 2:17)
1 (Phil. 3:13)
2 (Col. 2:17)
4 (Col. 2:13, 20)

D. FEATURES (15)

1-4 (in any order) Ephesians, Colossians, Philippians, Philemon
(Turn to page 55 to check explanation.)

5. Phil. (Text p. 57)
6. Col. (Text p. 57)
7. Eph. (Text p. 57)
8. Philem. (Text p. 57)
9. Eph. (4:3-4)

10. Phil. (Text p. 57)
11. Col. (1:18)
12. Phil. (4:4)
13. Eph. (2:8)
14. Col. (2:17)
15. Philem. (10)

UNIT 3: OTHER PAULINE LETTERS

OBJECTIVES

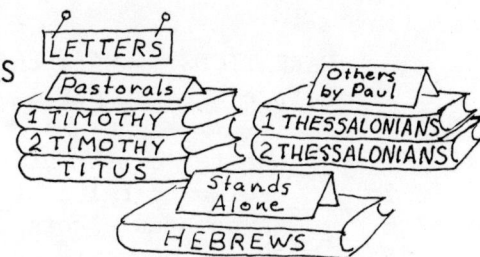

Upon the completion of Unit 3, you will be able to:

1. State the major headings in an outline of each of the six Letters in this unit.

2. Identify at least four individuals and one group from their descriptions or activities.

3. Identify three places from their descriptions.

4. Associate at least 20 partial teachings with their conclusions or descriptive phrases.

5. Identify at least 10 items as distinguishing features of a particular Letter or group of Letters.

Now begin the pre-test for this unit.

PRE-TEST FOR UNIT 3: OTHER PAULINE LETTERS

A. STRUCTURE: Write the number of each Letter in the blank before the major headings for that Letter.

_____ Jesus as Son and High Priest;
Necessity of Faithfulness

_____ Sound Teaching; Instruction
for Ministers and Leaders

_____ Maintenance of Contact; Exhortation;
Information and Requests

_____ Thanksgiving; Day of the Lord;
Don't Quit Work

_____ Sound Doctrine;
Church and Community

_____ Paul's Experience; Paul's Exhortation;
Paul's Farewell

1. First Thessalonians
2. Second Thessalonians
3. First Timothy
4. Second Timothy
5. Titus
6. Hebrews

B. NARRATIVES: Write the number of each person or place on the blank
    before the ONE phrase most closely associated with it.

1. _____ Where Jewish Christians were to be rebuked   1. Paul
2. _____ Followed rules of those who rejected truth   2. Timothy
3. _____ Appointed elders in every town   3. Titus
4. _____ Where converts were called exemplary   4. Silas
5. _____ Told to order halt of false teachers   5. Thessalonians
6. _____ Worked day and night   6. Jewish Christians
7. _____ At Thessalonica with Paul   7. Ephesus
8. _____ Timothy urged to stay there   8. Crete
9. _____ Faithful in spite of persecution   9. Thessalonica

C. TEACHINGS: Circle the letter of the ONE BEST answer to each.

1. In First Timothy there are instructions for ALL of the following EXCEPT:
    a. Pray for all men.
    b. Women, be quiet in church.
    c. Men, study God's Word.
    d. Pray for those in authority.
    e. Test church helpers before they serve.

2. The author of Second Timothy says the Good News is that:
    a. Gentiles have replaced the Jews as God's people.
    b. God treats all men alike.
    c. Jesus died for men.
    d. Christ ended the power of death.
    e. God came to man.

3. Jewish Christians were to be rebuked because:
    a. They argued with the Gentiles.
    b. They followed Jewish commandments.
    c. They were trying to keep Gentiles out of the church.
    d. They claimed that Paul was a false apostle.
    e. a and c

4. Concerning good works, the author of Titus said:
    a. Christians should give their time to them.
    b. Man is saved through faith, not works.
    c. Salvation is a free gift and cannot be earned.
    d. They will earn a reward for the doer.
    e. They should be the main concern of Christians.

5. Hebrews describes Jesus Christ as superior to ALL of the following EXCEPT:
    a. Angels
    b. Demons
    c. Moses
    d. Abraham
    e. All things

6. Hebrews says the new covenant is better than the old in that it:
   a. Avoids animal sacrifice
   b. Was made by God
   c. Replaces the Law
   d. Is with Gentiles, not just Jews
   e. Brings a Kingdom which will last

7. Abraham demonstrated his faith by:
   a. Being obedient to death
   b. Trusting God's promise of children in old age
   c. Killing his son at God's command
   d. Digging a well in the desert
   e. Obeying God's command to marry

8. The highest priestly order was:
   a. The order of Aaron
   b. The order of angels
   c. The Levites
   d. The order of Melchizedek
   e. The temple priests at the time of David

Write the number of each partial teaching on the blank before the ONE phrase with which it is most closely associated.

____ Acceptance of discipline
____ Win respect of unbelievers.
____ For those who act against gospel
____ Final rebellion
____ Source of evil
____ Never restrain.

1. The Lord's coming
2. The Holy Spirit
3. Earn own living
4. Love of money
5. Athlete
6. Law supports gospel.

____ Because of God's mercy
____ Anchor for our hearts
____ Responsibility within church
____ Man-made rules
____ Christians who leave truth
____ Give wisdom.

1. Scriptures
2. Being friendly to all men
3. No possible repentance
4. Mutual encouragement
5. Old covenant
6. Hope in God's promise

D. FEATURES: Write 1 Thess., 2 Thess., 1 Tim., 2 Tim., Titus, pastorals, or Heb. before the item(s) which distinguish that Letter, or the pastorals as a group.

1. _____ Church at Crete

2. _____ Church at Ephesus

3. _____ Church at Thessalonica

4. _____ Many Scriptural references

5. _____ Christ ends power of death.

6. _____ Were examples to other Christians

7. _____ Instructions to ministers

8. _____ Day of the Lord

9. _____ Love of money

10. _____ Superiority of Christ to angels

11. _____ If pseudonymous, may include fragments of a genuine Letter of Paul

12. _____ Earliest writing in New Testament

13. _____ No work, no food

14. _____ No repentance for fallen Christians

15. _____ Test church helpers.

ANSWERS TO PRE-TEST FOR UNIT 3

A. STRUCTURE (6)

6
3
1
2
5
4

B. NARRATIVES (9)

8
6
3
9
2
1
4
7
5

C. TEACHINGS (20)

1. c	5	2
2. d	3	6
3. b	6	4
4. a	1	5
5. b	4	3
6. e	2	1
7. b		
8. d		

D. FEATURES (15)

1. Titus
2. 1 Tim.
3. 1 and 2 Thess.
4. Heb.
5. 2 Tim.
6. 1 Thess.
7. Pastorals
8. 2 Thess.
9. 1 Tim.
10. Heb.
11. 2 Tim.
12. 1 Thess.
13. 2 Thess.
14. Heb.
15. 1 Tim.

PRE-TEST SCORES FOR UNIT 3

Category	# Correct	% Score	Directions
A. Structure	____	____	See chart below for 6.
B. Narratives	____	____	# x 11 = ___ + 1 = %
C. Teachings	____	____	# x 5 = %
D. Features	____	____	See chart for 15
Total (A+B+C+D)	____	____	# x 2 = %

Record scores on Unit 3 Growth Record page 136, and begin Unit 3 on page 99.

#	1	2	3	4	5	6	#
%	17	33	50	67	83	100	%

#	1	2	3	4	5	6	7	8	9	10	11	12	13	14	15	#
%	7	13	20	26	33	40	47	53	60	67	73	80	87	93	100	%

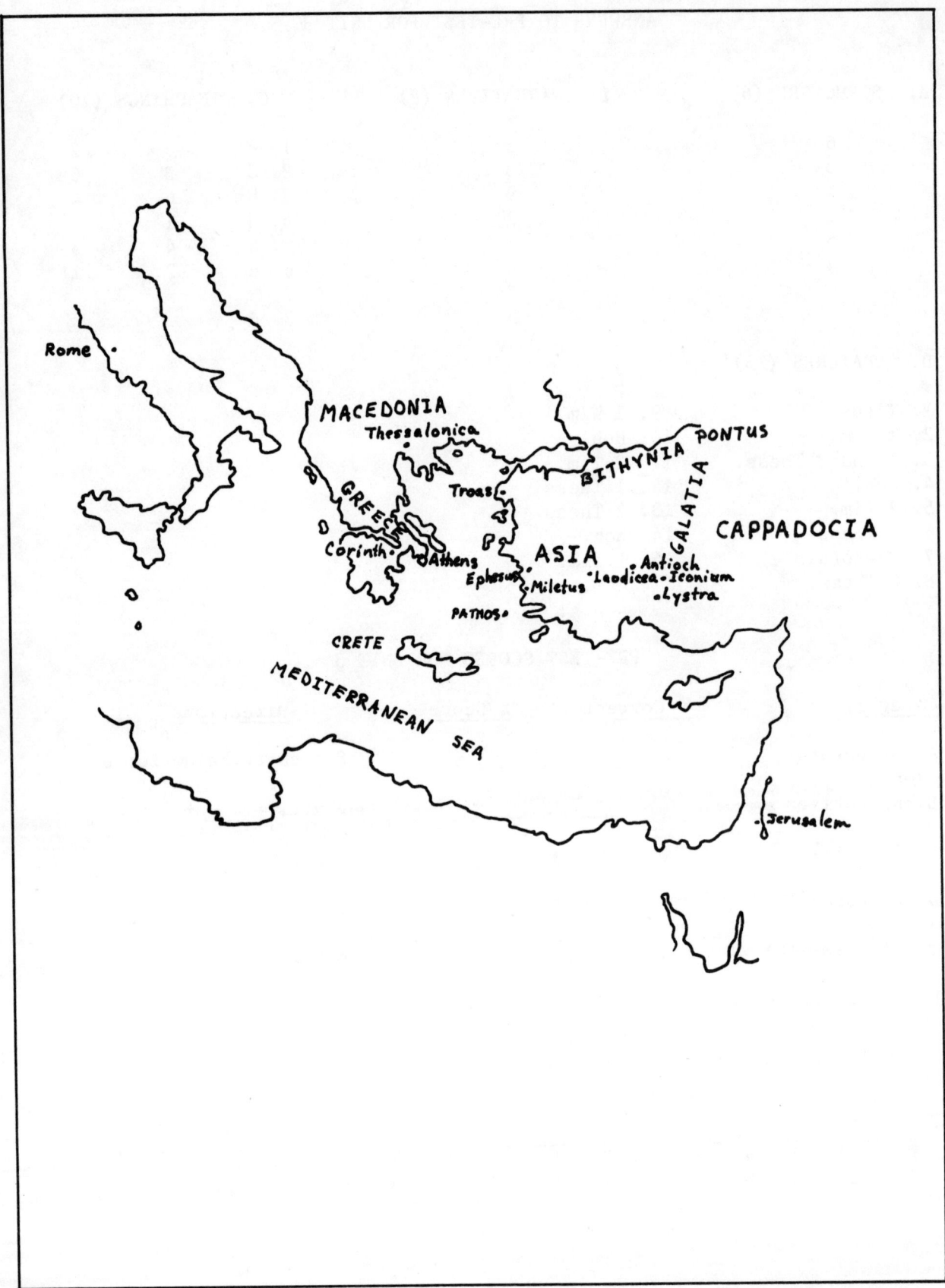

UNIT 3: OTHER PAULINE LETTERS
THESSALONIANS, PASTORALS, AND HEBREWS

This unit contains an ASSORTMENT of Letters including the EARLIEST and some of the LATEST of New Testament writings. First Thessalonians, the earliest, is the only one which almost all scholars agree was written by Paul. Along with Second Thessalonians, it is also the only Letter in this unit which was addressed TO A CHURCH.

The PASTORAL Letters deal with the problems of a pastor in guiding his congregation. They treat congregational matters of WORSHIP, DOCTRINE, and ORDER, and offer personal advice to a YOUNG MINISTER. These Letters may very well be among the last New Testament documents to have been written.

Hebrews STANDS ALONE in the New Testament. It is a SERMON or treatise, not a true letter. Hebrews did not claim anyone as its author or its specific recipient. It is an ANONYMOUS "letter."

This unit, unlike Units 1 and 2, treats more than one New Testament book in a single section on the page. The study arrangement is as follows:

Section 1: 1 Thess. and 2 Thess.

Section 3: 1 Tim., 2 Tim., and Titus

Section 3: Hebrews

The section charts and tests include the material from all the books in that particular section.

99

10 BACKGROUND OF FIRST THESSALONIANS

AUTHOR: Paul, undoubted

DATE: Ca. A.D. 50. The earliest of Paul's letters; therefore, the earliest writing in the New Testament (possible exception: Galatians)

READERS: The church (almost entirely Gentiles) which Paul had founded a few months earlier in Thessalonica

CIRCUMSTANCES: Paul had sent Timothy to get news of the young church. Timothy brought good news of their faith, but also news of persecution and the doubt raised by one member's death before the Lord's return.

30 BACKGROUND OF PASTORAL LETTERS (First and Second Timothy and Titus)

AUTHOR: Paul, according to the text, tradition, and some modern scholars. Most scholars, however, believe these Letters are pseudonymous (with fragments of a genuine Letter of Paul in 2 Timothy, perhaps).

DATE: About A.D. 63-67 if by Paul (after Roman imprisonment of Acts 28)
About A.D. 125 (?) if pseudonymous

CIRCUMSTANCES AND PURPOSE: If pseudonymous (definition on page 57), manuals of church order for congregations troubled by false teaching and needing rules for institutional life

If by Paul, instructions for younger missionaries he has left in Ephesus (Timothy) and in Crete (Titus); practical advice for their ministry

In either case, manuals for local church leaders: How to guard against heresy, how to preserve order and propriety in the congregation, how to conduct oneself

60 BACKGROUND FOR HEBREWS

AUTHOR: Anonymous. Surely not Paul, but probably (like Paul) a Hellenized Jew of the Dispersion who became a Christian

DATE: Uncertain, but no later than A.D. 95

READERS: Maybe Jewish Christians, as the title later added implies; maybe in Rome, as reference to "those in Italy" (13:24) suggests

CIRCUMSTANCES AND PURPOSE: A situation of extreme danger and persecution in which Christians were tempted to fall away from Christ and the church. This is a "word of exhortation" to be steadfast.

LITERARY TYPE: Not a letter or epistle, but a treatise or sermon

10 BACKGROUND OF FIRST THESSALONIANS

1. Written by _____ ca. A.D. _____

2. Thessalonians was ALL EXCEPT:
   a. Probably first writing of N.T.
   b. To a church Paul founded
   c. Probably first of Paul's Letters
   d. To a church Timothy founded
   e. To a new Gentile church

3. Timothy's visit to Thessalonica brought news of ALL EXCEPT:
   a. Their faith
   b. Their persecution
   c. False teachers
   d. Their doubts
   e. Death

Check previous page for answers, and then proceed to page 103.

30 BACKGROUND FOR PASTORALS

1. Date of writing was _____ or _____.

2. Authorship is:
   a. Anonymous
   b. Pauline
   c. Pseudonymous
   d. a or b
   e. b or c

3. The purpose of these Letters was to provide:
   a. A manual of church order
   b. Rules for institutional life
   c. Practical advice for ministers
   d. A guard against heresy
   e. All of the above

Check previous page for answers, and then proceed.

60 BACKGROUND FOR HEBREWS

1. Author was _____.

2. Hebrews was written to:
   a. Answer questions writer had been asked
   b. Urge Christians to keep faith
   c. Encourage during persecution
   d. Give rules for church order
   e. b and c

3. Hebrews is a:
   a. Treatise or sermon
   b. Report on the writer's work
   c. Letter to a church group
   d. Letter to a few individuals
   e. b and d

Check previous page for answers, and then proceed.

11   OPENING: First Thessalonians 1:1

12   MAINTENANCE OF CONTACT: EXTENDED THANKSGIVING

12A First Thanksgiving: 1:2-10
     READ: 1 Thess. 1--3

Paul was thankful for the faith, hope, and love of the new church at Thessalonica which made the Thessalonians examples to other Christians. What did people say the Thessalonians had done when Paul, Silas, and Timothy visited them?

****

31   OPENING: First Timothy 1:1-2

32   SOUND TEACHING. READ: 1 Tim. 1--3

1. Ordering Timothy to stop the false teachers in Ephesus, Paul told him that the Law supports the gospel. How?

2. When Paul, the "worst of sinners," was converted, he became an example for all who followed him. Whom did he trust to continue his ministry?

33   CONGREGATIONAL INSTRUCTIONS: 2--3

1. After urging Christians to pray for all men and especially those in authority, how did the writer say women should act?

2. The church leader was told to lead a godly life. To make sure that church helpers were of good character, what was to be done before they served?

****

61   PROLOGUE: 1:1-3

62   JESUS AS SON AND HIGH PRIEST: 1:4--10:18

62A The Person of the Son: 1:4--4:13

     READ: Heb. 1--2
     The theme is stated in verses 3 and 4.

1. In the first section the writer tells of Christ's superiority to angels. What do the angels do that indicates their relationship to Christ?

2. To whom does the writer refer in the Scripture (Ps. 8) about man being made for a little while lower than the angels, yet ruler over all things?

12A

1. They had turned from idols to serve the true and living God and to wait for Jesus to come.

****

32

1. The Law is made for those who do anything contrary to the gospel.

2. Timothy

33

1. They should be modest and quiet in church.

2. They were to be tested.

Now turn to Section Chart 3 on page 121, and complete blanks 1-5. Check answers on page 125. Study the corrected chart, and continue work on page 105.

****

62A

1. They worship him.

2. Jesus Christ

12B Paul's Ministry in Thessalonica: 2:1-12

What had Paul and his companions shared with the Thessalonians when Paul visited them?

12C Second Thanksgiving: 2:13-16

Paul was also thankful for their faith in the face of persecution.

12D Timothy's Visit and News: Third Thanksgiving: 2:17--3:13

Paul had sent Timothy to Thessalonica to find out if the Thessalonians had remained faithful during the persecution and to strengthen them. What news did Timothy bring back?

****

34 TEACHINGS: FALSE VS. TRUE: 4:1-5
READ: 4:1--6:2
The false teaching said it was wrong to marry and to eat certain foods. What is the true teaching?

35 INSTRUCTIONS FOR MINISTERS AND LEADERS: 4:6--6:2

1. In what way does the writer say that the good minister should be like an athlete?

2. Widows seem to have constituted a sort of religious order in the early church. What policy were church leaders told to follow concerning widows?

3. Hardworking elders were to receive double pay, but what were the leaders told to avoid in carrying out these instructions?

****

62A The Person of the Son. READ: 3:1--4:13

3. In the next section the writer tells of Christ's superiority to the patriarchs. Both Moses and Jesus were faithful to God. In what way is Jesus superior?

105

12B They shared the Good News
     and their lives.

12D The Thessalonians had
     remained faithful and thought
     well of Paul and Timothy.

Turn to Section Chart 1 on page 119, and complete blanks 1-3. Check answers on page 125. Study the corrected chart, and continue on page 107.

****

34   Everything God created
     is good, and so all is
     to be received with a
     prayer of thanks.

35

1.   He should keep himself
     in training for a godly
     life.

2.   Admit only widows over
     60 who really have no one
     to care for them; younger
     widows should remarry.

3.   Showing predjudice or
     favor.

****

62A

3.   Moses was a servant while
     Jesus is the Son.

106

13   EXHORTATION: INFORMATION AND REQUESTS

13A   Life That Pleases God: 4:1-12
      READ: 1 Thess. 4--5

How were the Thessalonians to win the respect of unbelievers and become independent?

13B   The Lord's Coming: 4:13--5:11

1. Some Christians were worried about relatives who had died before the Lord returned. What did Paul say to cheer them up?

2. How does Paul describe the day of the Lord's coming to most people?

13C   Instructions for Congregational Life: 5:12-22

1. What does God always want to see in a Christian in addition to prayer and thanksgiving?

****

36   THE TEACHING ABOUT RICHES.   READ: 1 Tim. 6:3-21

1. False teachers made money from religion. What does the writer think of those who love money?

2. Timothy's church in Ephesus must have had some rich members. What were the rich to be taught?

37   CLOSING: 6:21b

JUST FOR FUN!

The Letter to the Ephesians describes God's power as military armor. First Timothy advises the minister to keep himself in training spiritually as well as physically. Thinking of the athlete this time instead of the soldier, see if you can paint a picture of this training in godliness--in words and/or in sketches.

****

62B   The Son as High Priest: 4:14--10:18
      READ: Hebrews 4:14--5:10

1. Why does the author say Jesus is able to feel sympathy for sinful man?

2. High priests in ancient Israel were of the order of Aaron. To what order was Christ, the Son, said to belong as high priest?

13A By earning their own living and minding their own business

13B

1. He told them that those who died believing in Christ would be raised to life first when Christ returned, and then those who were still living would join them.

2. Like a thief in the night

13C

1. Joy

36

1. Their love of money is the source of all kinds of evil.

2. Not to be proud; to place their hope in God and to be generous

Turn to page 121 to fill in blanks 6-10. Check answers on page 125, then continue on this page.

JUST FOR FUN!

The young minister is given some specific advice in interpersonal relations: "Do not let anyone look down on you because you are young," and "Do not rebuke an elder man." Try to imagine two incidents, one involving each of these pieces of advice. Imagine the situation before, the actual encounter when the young minister follows the advice, and the situation after. Write down the dialogue for each encounter so as to focus on the problem and see exactly how the advice would apply.

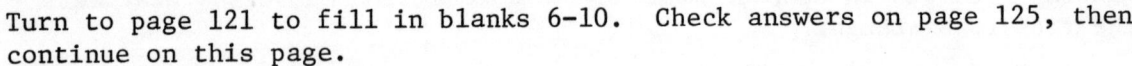

62B

1. Because he was tempted in every way as other men, although he did not sin

2. The order of Melchizedek (The quotation is from Ps. 110.)

108

13C Instructions for Congregational Life: 5:12-22

2. What advice did Paul give concerning the Holy Spirit?

14 CLOSING: 5:23-28

JUST FOR FUN!

Try to decode this statement:

    gni tir wtn tse ilr ae = sna ino las seh tts rif

                                       Hint: ITISWRITTEN BACKWARDS

****

41 OPENING: Second Timothy 1:1-2

42 PAUL'S EXPERIENCE: 1:3-18
    READ: 1:1--2:13

1. Paul was in prison for the Good News. What does Paul say the Good News is?

2. Paul said he had been appointed to proclaim the gospel. What did he urge Timothy to do?

43 PAUL'S EXHORTATION: 2:1--3:9

1. In exhorting Timothy to teach men who can be trusted to teach others, the writer gave three examples of accepting discipline in service. What is one example?

        ****

62B The Son as High Priest. READ: Heb. 5:11--6:20

3. The writer complained that he was handicapped because the readers were so slow to understand. What did he urge them to do?

4. Why is the writer so concerned about Christians falling away from the truth?

5. What is spoken of metaphorically as "an anchor for our hearts"?

13C

2. Not to restrain the Holy Spirit

Turn to Section Chart 1 on page 119, and complete blanks 4-10. Check answers on page 125. Study the corrected chart, and continue working on this page.

JUST FOR FUN!

Before you start 2 Thessalonians, why not try this? Read Acts 17:1-9 which tells of Paul's founding the church at Thessalonica, and reread 1 Thess. 1:14-15.

Assume you are a reporter on an assignment to cover a new way-out group in California. You witness a scene which arouses mob violence. Write the story trying to parallel the facts given in the New Testament.

****

42

1. Christ had ended the power of death.

2. To keep the good things entrusted to him ("Keep the faith.")

43

1. A soldier refrains from civilian life to please his commander; an athlete obeys the rules; a hard-working farmer should have first share of the harvest.

****

62B

3. To move on to mature teaching

4. Because once they had known God's Word and fallen away, he said it was impossible to bring them back to repent again.

5. Hope in the promise of God

110

20 BACKGROUND OF SECOND THESSALONIANS

AUTHOR: Paul, debated. Alternative: Pseudonymous

DATE: If by Paul, A.D. 51; if pseudonymous, A.D. 70-100

READERS: Church in Thessalonica (perhaps wider reading if pseudonymous)

CIRCUMSTANCES AND PURPOSE: The church misunderstood Paul's teaching about the Lord's coming. Some members claimed he had already come and others, expecting him any moment, stopped working. The Letter was written to clear up confusion and send people back to work.

****

43 PAUL'S EXHORTATION: 2:1--3:9 (cont.)
    READ: 2:14--4:22

2. How is the Christian teacher to deal with those who want to argue?

3. What kind of men should Christians avoid in the last days?

44 PAUL'S FAREWELL: 3:10--4:18

1. What does the writer say about the origin of the Scriptures, and what they are capable of doing for a man?

2. What time did Paul say had come for him?

45 CLOSING: 4:19-22

****

62B The Son as High Priest. READ: Heb. 7:1--10:18

6. Why was Christ's priesthood called superior when he was not descended from a tribe of priests?

7. What is the difference between the old and new covenants and their priesthoods?

20 BACKGROUND OF SECOND THESSALONIANS

1. ALL of the following might apply to the Letter EXCEPT:

   It was written:
   a. Anonymously
   b. By Paul
   c. By a later Christian
   d. To the Thessalonian church
   e. To a Gentile church

2. The Letter tried to clarify:
   a. The date of the resurrection
   b. The identity of the Wicked One
   c. The way to earn a living
   d. Signs of the Lord's coming
   e. b and d

Check information on previous page for answers, and proceed.

****

43

2. He should not argue, but be kind and gentle as he corrects his opponents.

3. Those who love pleasure rather than God

44

1. They were inspired by God and could give a man wisdom that leads to salvation and equip him to do every kind of good work.

2. The time to leave this life

Turn to page 122, and complete blanks 1-8 on Section Chart 4. Check answers on p. 125. Study the corrected chart, and turn back to p. 113 for "Just for Fun."

****

62B

6. Because he is of the order of Melchizedek who was superior to Abraham and the Levitical priesthood

7. The old involves man-made rules and cannot perfect man. Christ's priesthood and sacrifice once and for all is superior and allows him to guarantee the new covenant. (or in your words)

Turn to Chart 6 on p. 124, and complete blanks 1-5. Check answers on page 125. Study the corrected chart, and turn back to page 113.

21 OPENING: Second Thessalonians 1:1-2

22 THANKSGIVING AND PRAYER. READ: 2 Thess. 1:1--2:12

1. Christians in Thessalonica were experiencing persecution and suffering. In those circumstances, what was increasing in the Thessalonians for which Paul thanked God?

2. How did Paul show other churches his appreciation for the Thessalonians?

23 INSTRUCTION: THE DAY OF THE LORD: 2:1-12

1. What confused the Thessalonians?

2. What will happen before the Lord's return?

****

JUST FOR FUN!

Before you start Titus, take another look at 2 Tim. 1:3-7 and 3:10-11. Maybe you can do some detective work. How long would you say the writer had known Timothy? Do you think the mother and grandmother are alive at the time of writing? Read Acts 16:1-3 to compare. You may also want to look at Acts 14:8-21 which tells of Paul's first visit to Lystra when he probably met Timothy and his mother.

Knowing that many scholars think this Letter was written by a later-day Paul to a Timothy of another generation, you might reflect upon the picture of Timothy's ancestry in Acts and the mixture of Jews and Gentiles in the church of the early second century. Does the writer take a positive or a negative view of the church's Jewish heritage?

****

JUST FOR FUN!

Before starting the next major division of Hebrews, try this puzzle. Identify these scrambled words from Hebrews. Take one letter from the first word or phrase in each pair, and add it to the second. THEN rearrange the letters in each word or phrase to form a word important in Hebrews. (The result <u>for each case</u> will be two single words related to each other in Hebrews.)
Ex. As some - Brahma = Moses - Abraham

1. Stripes - No
2. Civil Zeal "T" - He licked me
3. Glances - Shirt
4. "Deer" fun - Refusing

22

1. Faith and love

2. He boasted of their endurance.

23

1. Claims of some that the Day of the Lord had already come

2. The final rebellion when the Wicked One will appear and oppose everything men consider divine

Turn to Section Chart 2 on page 120, and complete blanks 1-5. Check answers on page 125, and continue on page 115.

****

JUST FOR FUN!

You may like to locate or add on the map in Unit 2, page 56, the places you have just read about. In addition to the places referred to in Acts, you will want to add some of the places mentioned in Timothy. The Second Letter to Timothy mentions nine places. A number of places are described in the Good News (TEV) word list in case you are interested in looking them up.

Add to your list of persons both new facts about the ones you already have on your list and new names.

****

JUST FOR FUN!

Answers: 1. Priest and Son
          2. Levitical and Melchizedek
          3. Angels and Christ
          4. Endure and Suffering

24 SECOND THANKSGIVING AND PRAYER: 2:13--3:5
    READ: 2 Thess. 2:13--3:18

After urging the Thessalonians to stand firm, what does Paul ask them to do?

25 EXHORTATION: DON'T QUIT WORK: 3:6-15

1. Setting an example of working day and night to support himself, what did Paul tell the Thessalonians about those who did not work?

2. When Paul heard reports that some in the fellowship were lazy and meddled in the business of others, what command did he give?

3. How does Paul instruct the members to deal with a lazy member?

26 CLOSING: 3:16-18

****

51 OPENING: 1:1-4

52 SOUND DOCTRINE FOR CRETAN CHURCH.   READ: Titus 1--2

1. When Paul left Titus to appoint elders in every town in Crete, what were his instructions concerning the qualities of an elder?

2. Why does the writer say that Jewish Christians in Crete must be rebuked?

3. What does Paul say teaches all Christians to live self-controlled, upright, godly lives?

****

63 APPLICATION: NECESSITY OF FAITHFULNESS: 10:19--12:29

63A The Response of Faith: 10:19-39
    READ: 10:19--12:11

What is a Christian's responsibility to others in the fellowship?

63B Forerunners in Faithfulness: 11:1--12:11

1. The writer cites many examples of faith in the Old Testament. Can you remember two of the ways in which Abraham showed faith?

2. What greater example of faith does the writer describe?

3. What good does the writer say will come from endurance of suffering?

24 To pray that the gospel will continue and that Paul and his companions will be rescued from wicked men

25

1. "Whosoever doesn't work, doesn't eat."

2. To lead orderly lives and to work to earn a living

3. They should have nothing to do with such a one so he will be ashamed, and they should warn him as a brother, not as an enemy.

Turn to Section Chart 2 on page 120, and complete blanks 6-10. Check answers on page 125, and continue work on page 117.

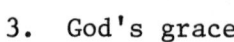

52

1. He must be without fault and hold firmly to the message.

2. So that they might have a healthy faith and no longer hold on to commandments of those who have rejected the truth

3. God's grace

****

63A Mutual Encouragement

63B

1. Obeyed God by leaving his country when called; trusted God's promise of having children in his old age; offered his son in faith God would raise Isaac from death

2. Jesus' faith and obedience to death on the cross

3. The peaceful reward of a righteous life

JUST FOR FUN!

In 2 Thess. the writer admonishes the lazy and the meddlers. They thought the Day of the Lord had come so there was no need to work, only to tell others what to do. They had a "good" excuse for taking the easy way out. Today in what ways do some people use their religion for immediate advantage instead of the long-range growth they claim for it? See how long a list you can make of such non-spiritual advantages which may prevent a person from true spiritual growth, usually without his knowledge.

Look again at your list. Do you find yourself anywhere in it?

****

53 RELATIONSHIP OF THE CHURCH TO THE COMMUNITY. READ: Titus 3

1. The Christians were told to submit to authorities. Why were they told to be peaceful and friendly to all men?

2. To what should Christians give their time?

54 CLOSING: 3:12-15

JUST FOR FUN!

Draw a line under a name (person or place) from the pastoral Letters hidden in each sentence. Ex. It's always in the past or always in the future. (pastoral)

1. I like the car, but it uses too much gas.
2. Is your mufti mothy, soldier?
3. With music, retention is greater.
4. Yep, he's useful, all right!
5. They keep a Ulysses picture on the mantel.

****

63C Exhortation and Warning: 12:12-29
     READ: Heb. 12:12--13:25

   What is the difference between that which is received under the new and old covenants?

64 CONCLUSION: 13:1-25

   What statement does the writer make about Jesus Christ?

JUST FOR FUN!

The Day of the Lord was widely discussed in the early church. Today we hear a lot about a possible end of the earth from physicists, ecologists, biologists, military experts, and statesmen. How is such talk similar to the New Testament, and what are the good effects in each case? What are the bad effects of such talk? What cure for these ill effects is available to the Christian? You may want to make a chart showing the various causes, bad effects on different age groups, and the available "cures" both for causes and for symptoms.

Take Section Test 1 on page 126.

****

53

1. Because they used to be hateful and have been made right with God only through God's grace

2. Doing good works

JUST FOR FUN!

Answers: 1. Titus   2. Timothy   3. Crete

            4. Ephesus   5. Paul

Turn to page 123 to complete blanks 1-7 on Section Chart 5. Check answers on page 125. Study all three pastoral letter charts, then take Section Test 2 on page 128.

****

63C

    Under the old, men received created things which will be removed. Under the new, men who listen to God receive a Kingdom that cannot be shaken.

64

    "Jesus Christ is the same yesterday, today, and for ever."

Turn to Section Chart 6 on page 124, and complete blanks 6-8. Check answers on page 125. Study corrected chart, and take Section Test 3 on page 130.

SECTION CHART 1: FIRST THESSALONIANS

OPENING

CONTACT: THANKSGIVING: 1--3

Exemplary Converts

with faith love and hope

Turned from

(1) _____ to _____

Paul the Missionary

in face of

(2) _____

=NEWS=

Timothy reports: Thessalonians have:

(3) _____

and _____

EXHORTATION AND INFORMATION: 4--5

(4) _____ that pleases God

Win respect:

Mind own business

(5) _____ own living

The Lord's

(6) _____

(7) _____
raised first

(8) _____
meet Lord

Surprise to most
Expected by:

(9) _____

Congregational Life

At all times ... pray, give thanks, and be

(10) _____

Be open to the

(11) _____

Having Faith, Love, and Hope

CLOSING

Check answers on page 125, and study corrected chart.

SECTION CHART 2:   SECOND THESSALONIANS

OPENING 1:1-2

THANKSGIVING AND PRAYER: 1:3-12

Thanks that
Thessalonians
are increasing in

(1) _____
      and
(2) _____

Paul (3) _____
of their endurance
of suffering

Coming:
God's righteous
JUDGMENT

May God
complete your
work of faith.

DAY OF THE LORD: 2:1-12

Not (4) _____

First:
Final rebellion
and appearance of

(5) _____

DON'T BE CONFUSED!

THANKSGIVING AND PRAYER: 2:13--3:5

Thanks for
Thessalonians

STAND FIRM!

Blessing

Blessing

Pray for (6) _____
that the message will

(7) _____

DON'T QUIT WORK!   3:6-15

Paul's Example:

Worked day and night

No work, no (8) _____

Lazy ones: Work!

Shun the (9) _____
  but treat as a

(10) _____

CLOSING: 3:16-18

Check answers page 125, and study corrected chart.

SECTION CHART 3: FIRST TIMOTHY

TEACHING	Minister	Members	Leaders

False:
DANGER STOP

True:
Supported by
(1) _____

Paul:
An example

(2) _____:
Take over.

ooooooooooooooooo
o SOUND TEACHING o
o   ch. 1   o
ooooooooooooooooo

---

ooooooooooooooooooooooooooooo
o CONGREGATIONAL INSTRUCTIONS o
o   ch. 2--3   o
ooooooooooooooooooooooooooooo

Pray for all men.

(3) _____
Be modest and

SHH!

Leaders:
live a

(4) _____
    life.

Helpers:
(5) _____
    first!

---

ooooooooooooooooo
o FALSE VS. TRUE o
o   ch. 4:1-5   o
ooooooooooooooooo

False:
Bad:

True: Good!
Eat and

(6) _____

Good minister:
In training
for

(7) _____

ooooooooooooooooo
o INSTRUCTIONS o
o FOR MINISTERS o
o AND LEADERS   o
o chs. 4:6--6:2 o
ooooooooooooooooo

Help good
(8) _____
who are old
and destitute.

Reward hard
workers, but
avoid
favoritism.

Teach the faith.
True riches, but

(9) _____ of
is source of

ooooooooooooooooo
o ABOUT RICHES o
o   ch. 6:3-21 o
ooooooooooooooooo

The rich:

Place hope in
God and be

(10) _____

Check answers p. 125, and study corrected chart.

SECTION CHART 4: SECOND TIMOTHY

OPENING: 1:1-2

PAUL'S EXPERIENCE: ch. 1

For the gospel

(1) _____ of

Ended by:

Paul:
(2) _____
the gospel

Timothy:
(3) _____ the faith.

PAUL'S EXHORTATION: 2:1--3:9

Accept
(4) _____
in service

to receive reward.

Christians:

Endure!

to live with

Christ

Christian Teacher:

(5) _____
quarrels.

Correct gently.

Avoid men who love

(6) _____ not God.

PAUL'S FAREWELL: 3:10--4:18

Scriptures bring wisdom,
(7) _____
and equipment for good works.

Timothy:

Preach!

Paul:

It's time for me to:

(8) _____

CLOSING: 4:19-22

Check answers on page 125, and study corrected chart.

122

SECTION CHART 5: TITUS

OPENING 1:1-4

SOUND DOCTRINE: ch. 1--2

Elders in every town:

Without fault
with firm
(1) _____

CRETE

God's grace instructs
all men to be

(5) _____
upright, and godly.

(2) _____
the false teachers, especially

(3) _____ Christians.

False teaching for

(4) _____

TITUS:

Use full authority!

CHURCH--COMMUNITY: ch. 3

Submit to

(6) _____

Be peaceful and friendly
to all men.

Because of God's grace

Do (7) _____

CLOSING: 3:12-15

Check answers on page 125, and study corrected chart.

123

SECTION CHART 6: HEBREWS

PROLOGUE: 1:1-3

DOCTRINE: chs. 1--10

JESUS THE SON: 1--3

Superior to:

(1) _____ and (2) _____

JESUS THE HIGH PRIEST
4:1--10:18

Sympathy for sinful man because:

(3) _____ as man is.

No (4) _____ possible
for Christians who leave Christ.

Order of (5) _____
forever

APPLICATION: chs. 10--13

NEED FOR
F
A
Response   I   Forerunners in Faith
T
Come to God   H
in Faith   F   (7) _____
U   of suffering leads
L   to righteous life.
Christians: N
E   Exhortation and Warning
Give   S
S   Old Covenant: Can be shaken.
(6) _____   New Covenant: (8) _____
encouragement.

CONCLUSION: ch. 13

Jesus Christ: the same   yesterday, today, and always

Check answers on page 125, and study corrected chart.

ANSWERS TO SECTION CHARTS

Sect. Chart 1
 1 Thess.

1. Idols to God
2. Persecution
3. Faith and love
4. Life
5. Earn
6. Coming
7. Dead
8. Living
9. Believers
10. Joyful
11. Spirit

Sect. Chart 2
 2 Thess.

1. Faith
2. Love
3. Boasts
4. Yet come
5. Wicked One
6. Us
7. Spread rapidly
8. Eat (food)
9. Lazy
10. Brother

Sect. Chart 3
 1 Tim.

1. Law
2. Timothy
3. Women
4. Godly
5. Test
6. Give thanks
7. Godliness
8. Widows
9. Love
10. Generous

Sect. Chart 4
 2 Tim.

1. Power
2. Preach
3. Keep
4. Discipline
5. Avoid
6. Pleasure
7. Salvation
8. Leave this life

Sect. Chart 5
 Titus

1. Faith
2. Rebuke
3. Jewish
4. Money
5. Self-controlled
6. Authorities
7. Good works

Sect. Chart 6
 Hebrews

1. Angels
2. Moses (patriarchs)
3. Tempted
4. Repentance
5. Melchizedek
6. Mutual
7. Endurance
8. Lasts forever

SECTION TEST 1: THESSALONIANS

A. STRUCTURE: Fill in the blanks in the following outlines.

First Thessalonians

I. (1) _____

II. (2) _____
   A. Life That Pleases God
   B. (3) _____
   C. Instructions for Congregational Life

Second Thessalonians

I. Thanksgiving and Prayer
II. Instructions: (4) _____
III. Second Thanksgiving and Prayer
IV. (5) _____

B. NARRATIVES: Write the number of each person on the blank before the phrase most closely associated with that person. Use each name ONCE and ONE name TWICE.

____ Returned to Thessalonica   1. Paul
____ Worried at deaths before Lord's coming   2. Timothy
____ Worked day and night   3. Silas
____ Helped establish the church at Thessalonica   4. Thessalonians
____ Brought news of continued faith

C. TEACHINGS: Circle the letter of the ONE BEST answer.

1. Paul told the Thessalonians to mind their own business and earn their own living:
   a. So they would no longer be a burden to Judean churches
   b. So they would become independent
   c. So unbelievers would respect them
   d. Because he had reports of their laziness and meddling
   e. b, c, and d

2. Paul says that at the Lord's coming ALL of the following will be true EXCEPT:
   a. Many will be converted
   b. Christians will be prepared.
   c. Christians will have faith, love, and hope.
   d. Most people will be unprepared.
   e. The living will meet the Lord after the dead do.

3. Concerning the Holy Spirit, Paul says:
   a. To pray regularly to the Spirit
   b. Not to restrain the Spirit
   c. That the Spirit will come like a thief in the night
   d. No one should expect the Spirit.
   e. Everyone has received the Spirit.

4. Before the Lord returns Paul says ALL of the following will occur EXCEPT:
   a. A final rebellion
   b. Satan will appear.
   c. Some will become wealthy at the expense of others.
   d. The Wicked One will oppose what men consider divine.
   e. Many will be deceived.

5. Concerning work Paul told the Thessalonians ALL of the following EXCEPT:
   a. He who doesn't work doesn't eat.
   b. He had heard that some of them were lazy.
   c. To warn the lazy brother and make him ashamed
   d. To remove from the fellowship the lazy ones who refuse to work
   e. Not to treat the lazy brother like an enemy

D. FEATURES: Write 1 Thess. or 2 Thess. before five of the following items which distinguish either book from other Letters.

1. ____ Put right with God through faith
2. ____ Confusion about the Lord's coming
3. ____ Worry about death of relatives
4. ____ Unity of the body
5. ____ Example to other Christians
6. ____ May be more than one letter
7. ____ Some lazy members
8. ____ Christ in first place
9. ____ Persecuted as the Judeans had been
10. ____ Abraham's faith

Check answers on page 132, and compute your scores below. Then enter your scores on the Unit Growth Record on page 136. After reviewing any items you missed, begin Pastoral Letters on page 101.

Category	# Correct	% Score	Directions
A. Structure	____ = ____		# x 20 = %
B. Narratives	____ = ____		# x 20 = %
C. Teachings	____ = ____		# x 20 = %
D. Features	____ = ____		# x 20 = %
Total (A+B+C+D)	____ = ____		# x 5 = %

SECTION TEST 2:   PASTORALS

A. STRUCTURE: Fill in the blanks in these outlines.

   First Timothy

   I.   (1) _____

   II. Congregational Instructions

   III. Teaching: False Versus True

   IV. Instructions for (2) _____
        _____

   V.   The Teaching About Riches

   Second Timothy

   I.   Paul's Experience

   II. Paul's (3) _____

   III. Paul's (4) _____

   Titus

   I.   Sound Doctrine
   II. Church (5) _____

B. NARRATIVES: Write the number of the name of each person or place on the blank before the ONE phrase with which it is most closely associated.

   ____ Timothy's church
   ____ Told to rebuke Jewish Christians
   ____ To carry on Paul's work
   ____ The time had come to die
   ____ Titus' church

   1. Timothy
   2. Paul
   3. Ephesus
   4. Crete
   5. Titus

C. TEACHINGS: Circle the letter of the ONE BEST answer.

1. All of the following instructions are given EXCEPT:
    a. Christians should pray for all men.
    b. Women should be quiet in church.
    c. Men should teach their families to pray.
    d. Church leaders should lead upright lives.
    e. Church helpers should be tested before service.

2. Concerning money the writer says:
    a. Love of it is the source of evil.
    b. Money is a source of evil for many people.
    c. Christians should not seek money.
    d. Rich Christians should give most of their money to the poor.
    e. b and c

3. Paul mentions the hard-working farmer as an example:
    a. Of the responsibility for self-support
    b. Of the Father who works constantly for his people
    c. Which Christians should follow
    d. Of the way to success
    e. Of accepting discipline in service

4. In referring to others who want to argue, the writer says the Christian should:
    a. Prepare stronger answers ahead of time.
    b. Not argue with them
    c. Pray for them.
    d. Correct them in a kind way.
    e. b and d

5. In 2 Tim. Paul says of the Scriptures ALL of the following EXCEPT:
    a. They were planned before the world began.
    b. They were inspired by God.
    c. They can give a man wisdom.
    d. They lead to salvation.
    e. There is no exception, all the above.

Write the number of each partial teaching on the blank before the phrase which most nearly completes it or with which it is most nearly associated.

____ Supports the gospel   1. Rebuke to Jewish Christians
____ Christ ended the power of death. 2. Being friendly to all men
____ Since God loves even us   3. Good works
____ Rules of those who reject the truth 4. Good News
____ Use of time   5. Law

D. FEATURES: Circle the number of FIVE items which distinguish the pastorals from other New Testament Letters.

1. Written mainly as guidance to church leaders
2. Written to those undergoing persecution
3. "The source of all kinds of evil"
4. Most scholars do not think they were written by Paul.
5. Undoubtedly written by Paul
6. Qualifications of an elder
7. Many Old Testament references
8. Written to combat immorality in the church
9. A good minister is like an athlete.
10. Warmly personal

Check answers on page 132, and compute your scores below. Then enter them on the Unit Growth Record on page 136, and begin Hebrews on page 101.

Category	# Correct	% Score	Directions
A. Structure	____	= ____	# x 20 = %
B. Narratives	____	= ____	# x 20 = %
C. Teachings	____	= ____	# x 10 = %
D. Features	____	= ____	# x 20 = %
Total (A+B+C+D)	____	= ____	# x 4 = %

SECTION TEST 3: HEBREWS

A. STRUCTURE: Fill in blanks in this outline of Hebrews.

I. Jesus as (1) _____ and (2) _____

II. Application: Necessity of (3) _____

    A. (4) _____ of Faith

    B. (5) _____ in Faithfulness

    C. Exhortation and Warning

C. TEACHINGS: Circle the ONE BEST answer.

1. Hebrews describes Jesus as superior to:
   a. Men, angels, and spirits
   b. Angels, Moses, and Levitical priesthood
   c. Adam, Moses, and David
   d. All creation
   e. All of the above

2. The writer says that Christians who fall away from the truth:
   a. Should be made to see the error of their ways
   b. Should receive the prayers of the congregation
   c. Should be rejected by the faithful
   d. Can never be brought back to repentance
   e. a and b

3. A responsibility of Christians to each other is described as:
   a. Bearing each other's burdens
   b. Sharing possessions
   c. Loving one's neighbor
   d. Teaching each other
   e. Mutual encouragement

4. The new covenant is superior to the old for ALL of the following reasons EXCEPT:
   a. Old covenant is false.
   b. Old cannot perfect man.
   c. Old involves man-made rules.
   d. Christ's sacrifice was once and for all.
   e. Christ's priesthood allows him to arrange the new covenant.

Write the number of the partial teaching on the blank of the ONE phrase with which it is most closely associated, but use ONE number TWICE.

____ The same always	1. An anchor for our hearts
____ Tempted in every way without sin	2. Christ
____ Hope in the promise of God	3. Jesus' sympathy for sinful man
____ Obedient and trusting in God's promise	4. Abraham
____ Peace in a righteous life	5. Endurance of suffering
____ Order of Melchizedek	

D. FEATURES: Circle the numbers of five items which distinguish Hebrews from other New Testament Letters.

1. Anonymous
2. Written to those in extreme danger
3. Written by Paul
4. Written to instruct a new church
5. Many references to O.T.
6. Day of the Lord
7. Christ's superiority to angels and patriarchs
8. Melchizedek
9. Armor of God
10. Apostleship

Check answers on page 132, and compute scores below.

SECTION TEST 3 SCORES

Category	# Correct	% Scores		Direction
A. Structure	____	= ____		# x 20 = %
C. Teaching	____	= ____		# x 10 = %
D. Features	____	= ____		# x 20 = %
Total (A+C+D)	____	= ____		# x 5 = %

Enter your scores on the Unit Growth Record on page 136. After checking any items you missed, take the unit test on page 133.

ANSWERS TO SECTION TESTS

Test 1:   Thessalonians

A. STRUCTURE (5)

1. Maintenance of Contact: Extended Thanksgiving
2. Exhortation: Information and Requests
3. The Lord's Coming
4. The Day of the Lord
5. Don't Quit Work.

B. NARRATIVES (5)

2
4
1
3
2

C. TEACHINGS (5)

1. e
2. a
3. b
4. c
5. d

D. FEATURES (5)

2. 2
3. 1
5. 1
7. 2
9. 1

Test 2:   Pastorals

A. STRUCTURE (5)

1. Sound Teaching
2. Ministers and Leaders
3. Exhortation
4. Farewell
5. And Community

B. NARRATIVES (5)

3
5
1
2
4

Test 2 continued

C. TEACHINGS (10)

1. c   5
2. a   4
3. e   2
4. e   1
5. a   3

D. FEATURES (5)

1
3
4
6
9

Test 3:   Hebrews

A. STRUCTURE (5)

1. Son
2. High Priest
3. Faithfulness
4. Response
5. Forerunners

C. TEACHINGS (10)

1. b   2
2. d   3
3. e   1
4. a   4
        5
        2

D. FEATURES (5)

1
2
5
7
8

UNIT TEST 3

A. STRUCTURE: Fill in the blanks on the following outlines.

<u>1 Thess.</u>

I. Maintenance of Contact: (1) _____

II. Exhortation: (2) _____

<u>1 Tim.</u>

I. (5) _____
II. Congregational Instructions
III. Teaching: False Vs. True
IV. Instructions for (6) _____

V. The Teaching About Riches

<u>Titus</u>

I. Sound Doctrine for Cretan
II. Relationship of (8) _____

<u>2 Thess.</u>

I. Thanksgiving and Prayer

II. Instructions: (3) _____

III. Second Thanksgiving and Prayer

IV. (4) _____

<u>2 Tim.</u>

I. Paul's Experience
II. Paul's Exhortation
III. Paul's (7) _____

<u>Hebrews</u>

I. (9) _____

II. Application: (10) _____

B. NARRATIVES: Write the number of the name of each person or place on the blank before the phrase with which it is most closely associated. Use each name ONCE unless marked TWICE.

1. ____ Appointed elders in each town
2. ____ Confused about Day of the Lord
3. ____ Time had come to leave this life.
4. ____ Persecution of new church
5. ____ Titus' churches there
6. ____ Told to stop the false teachers
7. ____ Timothy's church
8. ____ At Thessalonica on first trip
9. ____ Sent to get news of Thessalonians
10. ____ Provided an example by his conversion

1. Paul (Use twice.)
2. Timothy (Use twice.)
3. Silas
4. Titus
5. Thessalonians
6. Crete
7. Ephesus
8. Thessalonica

C. TEACHINGS: Circle the letter of the ONE BEST answer.

1. The Thessalonians were worried because:
    a. Some relatives had died.
    b. Their leader was ill.
    c. Christ had not yet returned.
    d. Their neighbors rejected Christianity.
    e. a and c

2. Paul said the Thessalonians were like:
    a. Stars shining in the night
    b. The Judean Christians who were persecuted
    c. The Christians in Macedonia
    d. Jewels on a crown
    e. a and b

3. The Jewish Christians in Crete were to be scolded for:
    a. Worship of idols
    b. Rejection of Gentile Christians
    c. Obeying rules set by those who reject the truth
    d. Immoral ways
    e. Their lack of enthusiasm

4. Hebrews describes Christ as ALL of the following EXCEPT:
    a. Descended from a tribe of priests
    b. In the order of Melchizedek
    c. Superior to angels
    d. A guarantee of a better covenant
    e. The same yesterday, today, and always

5. According to a statement in the pastorals, the Good News is:
    a. Christ is in all.
    b. Gentiles are God's children.
    c. Christ ended the power of death.
    d. Man is good.
    e. Jesus died for others.

6. In Titus, Christians are told to spend their time:
    a. Earning their own livings
    b. Studying the Scriptures
    c. In prayer
    d. Doing good works
    e. Preaching the gospel

7. In 1 Tim. instructions concerning ALL of the following were given EXCEPT:
    a. Leaders should not be recent converts.
    b. Helpers should be tested before serving.
    c. Women should be modest and quiet in church.
    d. Men should show consideration for women.
    e. Christians should pray for all men.

8. The author of Hebrews says that Christ can sympathize with sinful man because:
   a. He once was one.
   b. He was tempted in every way that man is.
   c. He had a part in creating man.
   d. He loves all men.
   e. a and d

In each of the two groups, write the number of the partial teaching on the blank before the phrase with which it is most closely associated.

____ Do not restrain.
____ Source of all kinds of evil
____ Can give wisdom
____ Need for discipline in service
____ Warn as a brother
____ Before Lord's coming

1. Final rebellion
2. Holy Spirit
3. The lazy
4. Love of money
5. Athlete in race
6. Scriptures

____ Christians' responsibility
____ to each other
____ Must be an example
____ Support gospel.
____ Hope in God's promise
____ Christians who fall from truth
____ Christ's sacrifice once for all

1. Law
2. No repentance possible
3. Mutual encouragement
4. New covenant
5. Young minister
6. Anchor for our hearts

D. FEATURES: Write 1 Thess., 2 Thess., 1 Tim., 2 Tim., Titus, or Heb. on the blank before each item which distinguishes that Letter.

1. ____ Sent to Cretan church
2. ____ Earliest N.T. writing
3. ____ Members' deaths
4. ____ Confusion about Lord's coming
5. ____ Law supports gospel
6. ____ Acceptance of discipline in service
7. ____ Teaching ministers, members, leaders
8. ____ No work, no food
9. ____ Jesus the High Priest
10. ____ Many O.T. references

Check answers on page 136; compute scores below, and record on page 136.

Category	# Correct	% Score	Directions
A. Structure	____	= ____	# x 10 = %
B. Narratives	____	= ____	# x 10 = %
C. Teachings	____	= ____	# x 5 = %
D. Features	____	= ____	# x 10 = %
Total (A+B+C+D)	____	= ____	# x 2 = %

ANSWERS TO UNIT TEST 3

A. STRUCTURE (10)

(See headings and charts.)

1. Extended Thanksgiving
2. Information and Requests
3. Day of the Lord
4. Exhortation: Don't Quit Work
5. Sound Teaching
6. Ministers and Leaders
7. Farewell
8. Church and Community
9. Jesus as Son and High Priest
10. Necessity of Faithfulness

B. NARRATIVES (10)

4 (Titus 1:5)
5 (2 Thess. 2:2)
1 (2 Tim. 4:6)
8 (1 Thess. 2:14)
6 (Titus 1:5)
2 (1 Tim. 1:3)
7 (1 Tim. 1:3)
3 (1 Thess. 1:1, 9)
2 (1 Thess. 3:5)
1 (1 Tim. 1:12-16)

C. TEACHINGS (20)

1. e (1 Thess. 4:13-18)
2. b (1 Thess. 2:14)
3. c (Titus 1:10-14)
4. a (1:4, 5, 10; 12:2; 13:8)
5. c (2 Tim. 1:10)
6. d (Titus 3:8)
7. d (2:1, 9-12; 3:6, 10)
8. b (Heb. 4:15)

2 (1 Thess. 5:19)
4 (1 Tim. 6:10)
6 (2 Tim. 3:15)
5 (2 Tim. 2:3-5)
3 (2 Thess. 3:15)
1 (2 Thess. 2:3)

3 (Heb. 10:25)
5 (1 Tim. 4:12; Titus 2:7)
1 (1 Tim. 1:8-11)
6 (Heb. 6:17-19)
2 (Heb. 6:4-6)
4 (Heb. 7:27; 8:6)

D. FEATURES (10)

1. Titus (1:5)
2. 1 Thess. (p. 101)
3. 1 Thess. (4:13, p. 101)
4. 2 Thess. (2:2)
5. 1 Tim. (1:8-11)
6. 2 Tim. (2:3-7)
7. 1 Tim. (p. 121)
8. 2 Thess. (3:10)
9. Heb. (4:14)
10. Heb. (1:5-13; 2:6-8, 12, 13; 3:7-11, 15; 4:3, 7; 5:5-6, etc.)

UNIT 3 GROWTH RECORD

Category	Pre-test	Sect. 1	Sect. 2	Sect. 3	Unit	Growth
A. Structure	%	%	%	%	%	%
B. Narratives				xxxxxx		
C. Teachings						
D. Features						
Total (from other pages)						

(Instructions for use of Unit Growth Record are given in Unit 1, page 10.)